TRAVELLING BEYOND BORDERS

TRAVELLING BEYOND BORDERS:
FROM AFRICA TO AMERICA AND COUNTRIES IN BETWEEN
Copyright © 2023, Ida G. Boers
All Rights Reserved

Travelling Beyond Borders:
from Africa to America
and Countries in Between

Ida G. Boers
Atlanta, Georgia 2023

Dedicated to Hendrikus W. Boers
Beloved husband and best friend,
in memory

Cover photo: "Who is This?" Nice, France, 1959

Language Use

Many of the stories in this book take place in South Africa before, during and after Apartheid. South African names for geographical locations, and ethnic groups are used in context, consistent with the historical record. The author does sometimes quote other people who use racist language. Unfortunately this is unavoidable in an autobiography which includes South African history.

All the provinces were renamed after 1994, and several have been divided into smaller governmental units. The section of Transvaal where most of the South African stories take place is now Gauteng. A photograph of the Transvaal Highveld is now in Limpopo.

South Africa is slightly less than twice the size of Texas, with eleven main languages representing many more cultures. An example of the complex nomenclature of ethnic groups in South Africa is the use of "Kleurling" or "Coloured". Because "colored" is a racial slur in the United States, this may be confusing. The term refers to a specific ethnic group whose Khoi, European, Bantu and Malaysian ancestry, and Afrikaans language, reach back to the 17th and 18th centuries in the Dutch Cape Colony.

The established convention is to capitalize the names of ethnic groups, and to use lower case for race and color. Capitalization of terms like "Bantu", "Dutch", "Coloured", and "Indian" indicate that they are ethnic groups. References to racial categories like "black", "brown", and "white" may also aggregate several different ethnic groups, but are still in lower case. The spelling convention for part of the book is South African English.

Table of Contents

Preface 1
Introduction 3

Section I: From Holland to South Africa 5
    Travelling Beyond Borders 7
    My Father's Diary 1928.....15
    What's Behind a Family Name 21
    A Pioneer in Africa 27
    What's in a Name? A Story of Two Grandmothers 30
    The Station Master's Wife......35

Section II: Childhood on the Farm 39
    A New Country 40
    Guardian Angel....47
    A Day on a South African Farm 56
    Saara's Story ...61
    Little Buck...75
    Medicine Woman ...79
    The End of an Affair 83
    Getting Religion ...86

Section III: From High School to Nursing School 91
    Destiny...93
    The Girl with a Pearl Earring 100
    Remembering a Humble Man 103
    A Most Unusual Pet 108
    How I became a Nurse in South Africa 112

China Blue Cups 125

Section IV: Memories of WWII 133
Childhood Memories of World War II.....135
Three Blue Plates 143
Four Women and War.....149
Code Name "Big Cat"....153

Section V: From Marriage to the United States 155
The Proposal ..157
The Irony of Apartheid.....160
Welcome to America....164
A Radio Interview Brings Back Memories......168

Section VI: Travelling Companions 175
Appenzeller Cheese...177
Travelling Together...182
A Sabbatical Year in France 186
Dinner with a Priest.....194
The Charming French.....197
A Collection of Wine Labels....199

Section VII: After Hendrik........211
Who is This?....213
Remembering a Husband....219

Endnotes.....228
Acknowledgements....229

Preface

While my sisters and I collaborated to put this manuscript together for our mother, it came home to me that these stories weren't just the work of her later years. Even though we recognized many of them, loosely threaded in family lore, we'd been living with them all our lives without realizing it. They were inside of our mother's mind all along, waiting to be written down. If this book is the result of what has been happening backstage, I'd like to describe the backdrop of our family life.

It might be best to start this by way of linguistics to set the distinctive atmosphere. In one story the author writes, "Africa grabs hold of your heartstrings," and language is among its most binding connections. Most people on the African continent grow up speaking more than one language, and many more than two, indigenous as well as colonial. Our mother spoke High Dutch, the Groniger dialect, Afrikaans, English, as well as some Sesotho before she went to high school. Our father spoke Afrikaans, English and Zulu from childhood. Together our parents learned fluent German during our father's doctoral studies in the early 1960s, and French during a sabbatical in the 1980s. Our father was consummate in Ancient Greek as the basis for his research and teaching, and taught himself Portuguese for his work as a translations' consultant in Southern Africa in the 1970s. Of the two, our mother has always been the better linguist, soaking up languages by immersing herself in cultures, easily fluent and easily at home in the vernacular. These were the acoustics of our household.

Ida Gezina Hommes was born on a farm near Oberholzer, Gauteng, South Africa, on March 29th, 1936. Her book is dedicated to Hendrikus Wouterus Boers who was born on February 3rd, 1928, on a farm near Ermelo, Gauteng. They married on February 28th in 1959. After our father finished his dissertation at the University of Bonn in 1961, he accepted a faculty position at Emory University in 1962. He died in 2007. The narratives stretch over a century, including the beginning and end of Apartheid, the building and dismantling of the Berlin Wall, punctuated by many other events which shaped our mother's generation in the West. As she shows, it's impossible to chronicle her own life without the rich counterpoint of our father's. The stories themselves focus on the people who walked in and out across the smaller stage of our parents' lives.

As my sisters and I read through the stories, and queried our own social history and privilege, I also realized how much we took the binding ways of new communities for granted: unforgettable meals from recipes our mother gathered from friends who welcomed us in all the places we'd lived, drinking the wines our father chose as their best accompaniment. Like our parents, we also lived on three different continents. At home in Atlanta countless people wandered through our house and sat at our table to be sustained by our mother's beautiful hospitality, and our father's eager curiousity and conversation. Together they created an astonishing and diverse world for us: an international community of poets, scholars, clergy, activists, musicians, asylum seekers, relatives, and students. Ours was an extraordinary childhood.

Twenty-odd years ago, she started to research our family's Dutch history so that the three of us would understand where we came from, and to create some kind of sextant for her grandchildren to imagine an impossibly distant past. She wrote several extensive, precisely researched chapters which would one day become a book. It was after our father died that she joined a writers' group, and her friends and mentors there encouraged her to explore her gift of storytelling. This turned into a different kind of book than the one she originally envisioned for us, reaching beyond our family's history and the events of her time, to her own experience and personal reflections.

Greta Gezina Boers
Durham, North Carolina
August 2023

Introduction

How I Came to Writing This Book

On January 6th, 2007, my beloved husband, Hendrik, died in a tragic accident.

In a matter of hours, my life changed. Something I was totally unprepared for. Friends helped me through the worst in the beginning with advice such as getting more than one death certificate. A friend drove me to the Social Security office where I was told that I had to forfeit my Social Security income or Hendrik's. I chose his since it was more than twice my income. The title of the house was in his name so another friend took me to the courthouse in Decatur, Georgia, where I had to provide another death certificate to transfer the house to my name.

And more importantly going to the bank to close his bank account and transfer all the money and future income, like TIAA income (teacher's insurance) to my account. This way I was financially secure.

Through the years I often reflected on the 58 years of marriage to a remarkable man. Besides a fulltime job teaching at Emory University he managed to write six books, one of which, *What is New Testament Theology*, was translated into Dutch and Korean.

He was carpenter, electrician, and plumber all in one. In the spacious basement of our two story house he built two bedrooms with closets, and a bathroom that included electric lights and outlets. He put in a ceiling after he installed heating and air ducts to all the rooms. I did my share by painting all the walls and the ceiling in creamy white. Then we put down wall to wall carpets on the cold cement floor except the bathroom where he tiled the floor and part of the walls.

He became known as the "computer guru" for the School of Theology when computers gradually replaced typewriters, and where he guided all the secretaries and many faculty members through the process of how to use e-mail and writing articles instead of a typewriter, eliminating the use of paper.

When I had finally adjusted to a new life without Hendrik, I began to look for other ways of keeping busy. A friend told me about OLLI (Osher Lifelong Learning Institute) at Emory. I looked through the brochure and chose a creative writing course taught by Bard Lindeman.

On the first day, beginning September, Bard asked us to send him an e-mail of why we chose his class. I wrote him a brief history of my husband's death and that joining his class was the best move I made because it got me out of the house and focused on something else than my husband's death.

About a year later I sent him a story of my husband titled "Remembering a Husband." I wrote Bard that he should not consider this as a submission but only to show him how much I learned to write about personal issues. I was not yet ready to have a class discussion about such an emotional experience.

At OLLI I made a new set of friends: Trudy, Milt, Joe, and Richard. Later more friends joined our group, and we became a very compatible group of ten who shared stories and took turns hosting our twice a month meetings. We looked out for each other and most importantly we laughed a lot. After every meeting I felt inspired and ready to tackle the world.

Section I:
From Holland to South Africa

Travelling Beyond Borders

My Father's Diary 1928

What's Behind a Family Name

A Pioneer in Africa

What's in a Name? A Story of Two Grandmothers

The Station Master's Wife

Travelling Beyond Borders

My grandmother, Grietje Glas, was nine years old when Queen Victoria died in 1901 and twenty years old in 1912, when she married my grandfather, Engel Engels, just five months after the Great Ship Titanic disappeared into the dark icy waters of the Atlantic Ocean. Thereby hangs a story.

I was about fourteen when my mother told me about my grandmother who was passionately courted by a wealthy young man and who was so unhappy when she refused him in favor of my grandfather that he booked passage on the Titanic to begin a new life in America. He probably went down with the ship because she never heard from him again.

I was in the "and-they-lived-happily-ever-after" phase and although briefly interested in my grandmother's love life, that part of her story, like the Titanic, soon disappeared into the dark recess of my memory.

Then on September 1st, 1985, came the headlines: TITANIC FOUND! reviving the long forgotten story of my grandmother's suitor.

At that time I was deeply involved with tracing my Dutch ancestors and trying to write a family history. It was uphill work. There were only two of my grandmother's ancestors who had a bit of personal history and only because they were pastors. The rest were all farmers with no information other than who married whom and how many children they produced and who, for centuries, all lived and died within a fifty mile radius of each other in the province of Groningen.

The discovery of the Titanic was my Eureka moment. Though my grandmother was no longer living and I couldn't ask her about her suitor, I decided to make her the central figure—the connection point—of my family story. But even here I had not much to tell. How could I take scraps of information and quilt them together to create an interesting story when the only thing close to romantic drama was connected to a sunken ship? The rest of her life was anything but romantic. It was a life of hard work, care, and at times emotional trauma that she bore with quiet fortitude.

In one of our conversations she told me something of her childhood.

"My mother, Rienje Boerma, was a strict, serious, rather undemonstrative woman. In her mind a girl couldn't learn soon enough to become a good housewife. So, I had chores to do when I was still very little, maybe four or five years old. I had to help with cleaning, feeding chickens and gathering eggs, and as the eldest of six children I had to help take care of my siblings as well.

"My father, Reinder Glas, was the one who always hugged us," my grandmother continued. "He played with us: sneaked sweets into our pockets and told scary bedtime stories on cold winter evenings."

Then her life changed. Her parents sent her to live with an unmarried uncle, Gerrit Boerma and maiden aunt, Tjebbinna Johanna Boerma, siblings of her mother who still lived on the old family farm in a remote and poor farming community called Nordijk about thirty miles from her hometown of Midwolda.

"During the two years that I lived with my uncle and aunt," my grandmother told me, " I learned to milk a cow, and early every morning before I went to school, I had to hitch the blindfolded horse, Nellie, to the long handle of a large butter churn and lead her around and around to churn butter."

"Why did you have to blindfold the horse?" I asked.

"Because a horse without a blindfold would get dizzy walking in a tight circle," she explained.

"When that was done, I fed the chickens, put on a clean apron and clean clogs, and walked to school a few miles away.

"My aunt taught me to cook: she showed me how you can turn every part of a slaughtered pig into something edible. We canned vegetables and fruit during the summer—oh it was so hot and damp in that kitchen!—and stored in the cellar for the winter months.

Travelling Beyond Borders

"Those winter evenings were my favorite time of year when the three of us sat in the cozy kitchen talking and sharing stories while my uncle taught me to knit—"

"Your uncle taught you to knit?" I interrupted.

"Oh yes, it was a centuries old tradition among farmers: men knitted scarves and socks—you had to wear thick socks with wooden clogs—women sewed shirts and dresses. But it was my aunt who taught me to crochet: anything from bedspreads to beaded doilies to cover the milk jug.

"And on Saturdays after we had polished all the copper and silver, we gathered around the kitchen table with the two farmhands—they slept in the barn—to eat the traditional Dutch pea soup thickened with sliced sausage and chunks of potato. And for dessert we had thick buttermilk pancakes with homemade syrup. I was fascinated with how easily those farmhands—and my uncle—could put away up to six of those huge pancakes."

My grandmother ended our conversation with a wistful sigh. "I look back on those two years as the happiest of my childhood. I was treated like an only, much loved child and I was sad to leave them."

Later she showed me a small Bible with gold clasps containing only the New Testament and a Hymnal. "My aunt gave me this when I left. I want you to have it one day when I'm gone."

On the first blank page my grandmother had written: "Gift from my beloved aunt, Tjebbinna Johanna Boerma. Born 17 December 1864, died 12 October 1911."

On the next page I read: *The New Testament Faithfully Translated from the Greek Language into our Dutch Language as decreed by the States General of the United Netherlands during the Synod of Dordrecht*, (Dordt) 1618/19.

When I finally got the Bible some thirty years after her death in 1957, I made an interesting discovery. How I wished I could go back in time to tell her about it.

"Oma," I would say, "I found one of your ancestors in the small Bible you left me."

She would look surprised but then ask with a sly smile. "One of the Apostles was an ancestor of mine?"

"A little more recent," I would joke back, and tell her about her ancestor who was a delegate to the Synod of Dordrecht in 1618/19.

She probably had never heard of the Synod or know the history of the eighty-year war of ruling Catholic Spain against the increasingly Reformist Dutch people.

Her ancestor, Wibbo Hommens, was born about 1572 in the small village of Oostwold not far from the Monastery of Heiligerlee where the Spanish/Dutch war began in 1568.

His father, enamored with the teachings of Calvin, decided to send his son to the University of Heidelberg—the only Reformist University—to get a degree in theology. It was at a considerable risk of getting caught by roving Spanish soldiers and ending his life in a dungeon that Wibbo traveled across the Dutch border to Germany. But Wibbo made it safely to Heidelberg.

His first view of Heidelberg must have been breathtaking. Nestled in the Odenwald hills the town sloped down to the banks of the wide Neckar River. Behind it he could see the majestic Koenigstuhl (Kings Throne) Mountain rising 1500 feet into the sky. Dense forests surrounded the town, the weather was glorious, and there was peace. It was such a sharp contrast to his hometown, Oostwold, where the land was flat as far as the eye could see, the highest hill was a dike, and the landscape dotted with burned out homes and destroyed farms.

On April 14, 1593, Wibbo was officially admitted as a student of theology at the University of Heidelberg. All the classes he attended were conducted in Latin, a language in which he excelled. Even his name became Latinized to Wigboldus Homerus, a name he used from then on.

In 1594, only a year after he had left Groningen, the war there came to an end, and Groningen was officially declared Protestant while the war raged on in the rest of the Netherlands till 1648.

When he returned home five years later with a degree in hand, almost everything that reminded of Catholicism had been obliterated and people were slowly rebuilding their lives and war ravaged land.

In 1601 Homerus got the plum job as the first Protestant pastor of one of the largest churches in Groningen: the community of Midwolda. The Romanesque basilica built in the 13th century and dedicated to John the Baptist stood a majestic stone throw away from the farm where my grandmother was born and raised. Homerus also received his own official seal, depicting John the Baptist holding a lamb in his arms—as patron of the Midwolda church—and the name Wigboldus Homerus inscribed around it. He used this seal as signature for all legal and church documents. (Now housed in the city of Groningen Archives.)

Here my grandmother would interrupt me—"Wait! There was no church close to our farm, where did you get that from?"

"That's because it no longer existed by the time you were born," I would explain. "One of the four church towers—that could be seen for miles around—fell down in 1667, and the nave by that time was in serious disrepair. The years of repeated battering by hurricane floods had taken its toll on the old church. It had become a safety hazard. So on July 4, 1668, the Regents of Groningen, with some regret, decided to dismantle the church."

At this point I had to get back to the Synod of Dordrecht and tell my grandmother about her ancestor's role in it.

Homerus had become well known as a dedicated hardworking pastor, and when the Synod of Dortrecht was convened, chosen to be one of the delegates to represent Groningen Province. He was a member of a small committee of Latin experts whose task was to edit and finally approve all the notes written in Latin during the yearlong Synod and finally hand it over to the executive committee as an official published document.

I can imagine that my grandmother would not be very impressed with my story. It was understandable: events that happened so many centuries ago did not interest her very much when daily life brought more than enough to keep her thoughts busy. But her ancestor's blip of fame in the annals of Dutch Church history provided *me* with a small and exciting sparkle in an otherwise dull family history. What *might* have interested her is that he was the first to travel beyond the borders of Groningen and that she would only be the second, 335 years later. When my grandmother returned to her family in Midwolda, she attended what was then called a "Housekeeping School" where she learned, among other things, to care for the sick, until she met my grandfather at some social event. When exactly he seriously began to court her is hard to tell. With dark curly hair framing her lovely face, large hazel eyes, and gentle demeanor she had, no doubt, many suitors, among them the tragic Titanic fellow, vying for her hand.

My grandmother married into a family at a time when the size of a woman's dowry was a way to measure the wealth of her parents. Her two sisters-in-law each brought a profitable farm with a large two storied house. She brought a few pieces of furniture, bed linens and knew how to milk a cow.

She married the youngest of eight children, the sickly one. To paraphrase Jane Austen: It is a truth universally acknowledged that a single man of frail health and uncertain future as a farmer, must be in need of a wife who could nurse him in sickness and run the daily business of farm life. My grandmother fit the bill, but not only that, it turned out to be a happy love match.

My grandparents settled close to the town of Noordbroek (Northbrook), on a farm that was established in 1754; acquired by the Engels family in 1813 and a spacious two story house that was built in 1863. My grandfather added more bedrooms for the growing family and, remarkable for that time, installed a bathroom with shower and a separate flush toilet.

The farm flourished through the years as did the six babies—which some

Travelling Beyond Borders

local farmers humorously described as a bumper crop—who arrived one after the other, like clockwork. My mother was the second baby.

Meanwhile my grandfather's health did not improve. He was often ill, and my grandmother had not only the burden of nursing him, caring for small children, but also to supervise the daily work on the farm. She was exhausted.

After another month-long bout with pneumonia, the doctor advised that he and his family move to a warmer, drier climate, like South Africa. My grandfather took his advice seriously and in September 1927 set sail to find a farm somewhere in South Africa.

It was snowing on that day in late January 1928 when my grandfather's letter arrived to say that he had found and bought a farm in the Western Transvaal. She was to sell the farm in Noordbroek and everything on it; pack up some furniture (among them the large cabinet; a wedding gift from her parents when she married my grandfather, now in my living room) and other household goods; and bring their children to sunny South Africa.

I often wonder what went through my grandmother's mind when she read that letter. Did she look out the living room window and think, "I will never see snow again." Or when she looked around the living room, and saw the baroque mirror on the wall reflecting the snowy scene outside, the colorful orange, blue and beige Smyrna carpet covering the wooden floor, the elegant chairs on which only visitors sat, and think, "I have to leave all this: the comfortable house and my family, my friends . . ." and so much else she could not think of at that moment.

My grandfather's letter made the reality of what lay ahead sink in: they would settle on a stretch of treeless uncultivated land on the spacious Transvaal veldt, where the only available source of water was pumped from deep below the surface. There was no house yet, my grandfather wrote, "but I will build you one as soon as possible, and plant vegetables and fruit trees," he promised, as if he felt guilty for taking her away from her beloved country.

Then the sudden distant chimes of the church clock striking four times would remind her that it would be getting dark soon and her children were on the way home from school. I imagine that she went to the kitchen and, as a special treat, warmed up some milk flavored with aniseed, cut thick slices of Groninger spice cake spread with homemade butter, and tell them the news.

A light snow was falling—almost like a parting gift—on the day in early April in 1928 when my grandmother and her children waved goodbye to family and friends as the train departed from the Noordbroek station and headed for the Rotterdam harbor.

Settling in a new country in the first years was at times a near traumatic experience. The family had to adjust to a different climate, get used to a variety of people: white, black, brown, Indian, each with their own languages and customs. But as the years passed South Africa became their homeland and despite some setbacks brought many rewards.

When my grandmother died in 1957, a family friend and well-known historian, Jan Ploeger, wrote her obituary in a Groninger newspaper: "She was a generous hostess to many foreign visitors, a gentle guide to all her family and friends, and an example of fortitude and dignity during her often difficult life."

Little did she know that years later many of her grandchildren and great-grandchildren would follow in her footsteps and travel beyond the South African border and scatter like wind-blown chaff, to settle in foreign countries: New Zealand, Australia, Japan, Thailand, England, Holland, and the USA.

And not a single one of them know how to milk a cow.

My Father's Diary 1928

(How my father's diary helped me write my story)

I didn't quite know what to expect when my mother called me soon after my father's death to say she had found two of his diaries—1924 and 1928. Would I like to have them? "Oh yes!" I said. I was curious to find out what he was like as a young man. What did he do every day? What interested him? Particularly in 1928, an important year in his life.

The Dutch diaries were the pre-dated kind with just enough space between the days of the week to write a short paragraph. My expectations were severely disappointed at first when I discovered that he used the minimum of words — seldom using up the allotted space.

On Sunday January 1st, 1928, for instance, he writes: *Skating*. What can I do with a single word?

Suddenly I hear my father's voice. "Okay, I've given you a clue on how I spent my 22nd birthday, now use your imagination to create a story."

In that upper corner of Holland, the Province of Groningen, where my father grew up, the water canals are usually frozen solid during the winter months. Skating is a centuries old national sport where people can skate for miles on canals that snake passed farms, through villages, towns and snow covered countryside. I imagine that my father and his friends travel seven kilometers east from his hometown of Beerta towards a town on the German border. There they spend a pleasant hour or two drinking cups of steaming coffee and feasting on the traditional New Year's Day *Oliebollen* (deep fried raisin filled dough balls, sprinkled with powdered sugar), then skate back home.

Monday, January 2nd, three words: *Two laborers; veterinarian.* The last one gives a clue: farming. No need for imagination here.

Six centuries of farmer's blood flow through his veins. His ancestors lie buried in the rich clay soil where they plowed and planted and raised cattle—scattered within a thirty mile radius around his father's own farm. (I can imagine that his genes viewed under a microscope would show traces of clay, cow dung, and hay.)

Unlike his earliest traceable ancestor—born 1440—my father does not milk cows, shovel manure or harvests wheat with a scythe under the hot August sun. Instead, he attends agricultural college for a few years, comes back to his father's farm to learn the business of farming, and supervises farmhands who do all the work.

Except the plowing; that's his job. On Friday, January the 13th, he writes, *Tractor lessons.* Another clue: my grandfather, Eggo Hommes, is a forward thinking farmer; he has replaced the horse-drawn plow with a tractor that plows the land in half the time it took before. All ready for planting in the spring.

My grandfather also owns a car, a rarity in that area where many people still make do with horse and buggy to get around. On January 16th, my father writes: *New lamp auto, 6 liters benzene, 2 liters oil.* At a later date he writes: *Fixed a flat tire.* On a Saturday he takes his younger—developmentally handicapped—sister, Janny, for a drive.

On Wednesday January 25th he writes: *Sale of horses and cows, farm of Engel Engels.* A surprise! Engel Engels is my maternal grandfather. News travels fast in a farming community:

"Did you hear, Engels wants to emigrate to South Africa?" one says.

"He's already there looking at farms in the Transvaal. His doctor advised him to move to a warmer drier climate," explains another. My father and grandfather travel twenty kilometers to attend the sale.

Is my father thinking of emigrating too? Or just curious to see what a successful farmer has to offer? And does he meet his future wife on that day? Not likely; my mother is thirteen years old and in school.

On February 1st, my father notes: *Final sale on Engels farm.* Everything has to go: furniture, household goods, and farm implements including the old coach that stands forlornly in the barn. And the horses, Eddie, and Bles, that used to pull it.

The daily entries of farm life continue: farmhands are *weeding thistles* day after day (ironically, a profusion of thistles indicates rich well fertilized soil). The *Milk Inspector* comes to inspect the stable and dairy. It is required for all farmers who send milk to the milk factory in town, where it is made into butter, yogurt, and cheese.

A cow named *Hebe* produces a *bull calf. Sold for F11.00* (Florin) on the same day. Another, *Vesta*, produces a heifer *calf*. It stays. The dairy maid milks the first flow of milk—*biestmelk*—into a small container before the newborn calves get a turn. It's tradition: the fatty nourishing milk is used to bake thick fluffy plate size pancakes, served with homemade syrup. That's what the family has for supper.

(It was custom to give cows names. My father probably had a hand in naming some cows. *Hebe* is the Greek goddess of youth. *Vesta* is the Roman goddess of the hearth. Does naming cows after goddesses reveal a youth's quirky sense of humor or that his interest in mythology takes him a step too far? I will never know.)

On February 28 he writes: *Lecture on Immigration.* It's *Snowing* on April 18 and 19th. He takes an *English lesson 9-11am* on the 18th and on the 23rd. Do English lessons hint at thoughts about emigrating? It's important to know English if he plans to settle in a country like America, Canada, or South Africa. His diary reveals no such plans, yet.

But he does read Dutch translations of authors like Oliver Curwood, Jack London, and others. Charles Dickens doesn't interest him. Stories about far away countries like those of Norwegian author Sven Hedin, do. Hedin describes his adventurous travels—in three volumes—from North Pole to South Pole and every continent in between, in vivid—sometimes gory—detail. Among my father's boyhood books are Karl May's stories of Indians and the American Midwest, wedged between *Tarzan of the Apes* and *Uncle Tom's Cabin.* All these books reflect a young man's curiosity of life in other more exotic lands beyond the confines of his compact and staid mother country.

It's not all work and no play on the farm—where work begins at 4am to milk the cows and ends at 6pm when the second milking is done. He has an active social life. He plays tennis, goes to horse races and attends any musical event he can get to. He loves music, not the Beethoven and Bach that his piano teacher drilled into him, but the songs of Franz Lehar and the waltzes of Strauss.

On January 10th he and his father travel to the city to see Goethe's *Faust.* On April 3rd, Molière's *The Miser.* And once a month he and his friends go to a dance club, oddly named, *Never Mind.*

On June 5th he travels to Germany. He is fairly fluent in German. His sister Geertrui, who is working towards a PhD in German Literature at the University of Groningen, tutors him. He gets a chance to use it in Leipzig where he goes to the *Crystal Palace* for a variety show. On the 7th he goes on a bus tour through the city to see the *Battle of the Nations War Memorial of 1813* and the *Südfriedhof Crematorium.* Friday the 8th finds him in Dresden where he visits the museum and attends a play in the *Hoftheater.*

On Monday the 10th he is home, and back to work on the farm. The stable gets a thorough cleaning on the 19th, ready for the cows that are stabled there during the winter months. They spend the summer months in the pasture grazing, and also milked there.

June, July go by. In August harvesting begins; barley, ryegrass and peas are brought into the barn. The steam operated threshing machine threshes the harvested wheat. On Thursday September 13th it's, *everything inside.* Harvesting is done.

Travelling Beyond Borders

But there is no rest on a farm; there's a continual never-ending flow of work in the life of a farmer. So, on Monday the 17th plowing begins all over again to ready newly harvested land for the next planting.

Plowing is noted with boring regularity every day in early October. But on the 10th, there is a change. My father writes: *Decide Transvaal,* the words firmly underlined, twice. The suspense is over. He is going to emigrate to South Africa. An auspicious day? It's my mother's 14th birthday. And she's already there in the desolate place where he will finally settle as a farmer.

My father's decision to move to another country is not unusual. Many sons of farmers leave the farm to follow another career: they become lawyers, teachers, and mechanics or emigrate to other countries to seek their fortunes there. Lucrative farming in Groningen in the twenties is in decline thanks to the American Midwest that floods the European markets with cheaper grains and other commodities.

Meanwhile work on the farm goes on, also social events and English lessons. On October 22nd he travels to Amsterdam to file for immigration papers and get a passport. Is he excited? Anxious about the big step he is about to take? He resolutely keeps his feelings to himself.

November 1st he notes: *Geertrui passed doctoral exams with distinction!!!* The three exclamation marks express his joy. His older sister has been his best friend since early childhood, and he is very proud of her.

November is also the month that he visits friends and family to say goodbye. On November 16th he buys a camera. Other than noting that a cousin got engaged, the rest of November remains blank. He is seriously busy getting ready for his departure. On Monday December 3rd he and his father go to the bank in town.

Then comes the big day: on December 6th he gets on the train headed for Rotterdam, and from there, on the 7th, to Southampton, England. His parents take him to the station. They say goodbye with typical Groninger reticence: no overt display of emotions, no hugs, no tears—fully aware that many years may pass before they meet again. Eggo Hommes, whose warm and kind demeanor hides a sharp mind, clasps his only son's hand firmly as he says, "*Success mien jong.*" (Success, my son.) His mother brushes his cheek lightly with a kiss. The Groninger dialect she usually speaks in a clipped tone—which in his boyhood turned into a staccato tirade whenever he thwarted her attempts to punish him for his misdeeds—softens as she wishes him a safe journey.

Their love for him is expressed in other ways: a generous letter of credit from his father, hidden in his breast pocket with his passport. His mother's repeated question, "Did you pack everything on your list?" "Yes, everything," he assures her. Blankets, books, paper, pen and ink, several sets of underwear, suits, shoes, bars of tar soap, towels, camera, compass, a revolver, and bullets. (Does he anticipate adventures in the unknown country of wild animals and black savages?) Also a small sewing kit his mother presses into his hands at the last minute, ignoring the fact that he can't even thread a needle. All fill the two trunks that will accompany him on the ship.

After December 7th the rest of the diary is blank until December 23rd when my father arrives in Cape Town. And where another story begins.

My father is only 22 years old when he leaves the Netherlands for good. When he boards the ship in Southampton harbor, he does not yet know where he will settle in the Transvaal, but he is filled with ambition and self-confidence; ready to take on any challenges that life in a new country will present.

And that he will make good. Which, after some hefty knocks, he does.

What's Behind a Family Name?

My father, Jan Hommes, was a tall proud man. Some would say he had reason to be. He grew up in the Oldamt, a district in the Province of Groningen, where lived the highest concentration of wealthy farmers in all of Europe.

It was a series of unrelated events that brought about this wealth. When Napoleon's vast army marched through the Netherlands in 1812 on its way to Russia it left the country depleted of most of its resources and the inhabitants on the brink of starvation. Then cattle plague decimated the dairy industry of Groningen. This forced farmers to look for other ways to produce food to feed the hungry people.

Here Providence stepped in. Through centuries of repeated flooding of the low lying Netherlands, a thick layer of mineral rich sea clay was dumped on the Groninger land particularly in the Oldamt district. It was the ideal soil for planting food crops like wheat, oats and barley.

From about 1839 to 1877 top quality grains at premium prices poured across Groningen's borders into all corners of Europe. It brought about a profound change in the lives of many farmers in the Oldamt. They became the elite upper class, and their increased wealth allowed for a building spree of stately two story mansions furnished with oriental carpets, baroque mirrors, and fine china.

My father, the only son, grew up in such a house. He did not shovel manure, milk cows at four in the morning or plow the land. Farmhands did it all. Instead, his parents sent him on cultural trips throughout Europe to round off his education. Then to agricultural college to learn all about farming.

But by then farming in Groningen was not so lucrative anymore. The culprit was the grain producing American Midwest that used steamships to transport much cheaper grains to European markets. America also revolutionized farming techniques: from steel plows to steam operated threshing machines.

Groninger farmers tried to keep up with the changes but for many it was too late. The only way out for some of them was to take what was left of their fortunes, leave the Netherlands, and seek a new life elsewhere. Among those Groningers who chose to invest their money in South Africa, and settle there as pioneer farmers, were my father and maternal grandfather.

My father was a cocky self-assured 22-year-old young man when he arrived in South Africa in 1928. In the same year my fourteen-year-old mother and her family settled on a farm in the spacious Western Transvaal about two miles from my father's.

The first years were rough. Adjusting to a new country, different climate that required different farming methods, and a variety of cultures and languages took some time. But with self-assured determination, and wise counsel from his future father in law, my father finally got his dairy farm working. In 1934 he asked my nineteen-year-old mother to marry him. All he could offer her was a small house where a rug made of burlap bags covered the cement floor in the living room, and a wooden crate functioned as coffee table. She accepted. I was born two years later.

About the same time, gold was discovered five miles away from our farm. My father wasted no time to get involved in the flurry of urban development that followed. With a hefty loan from his father—which, in fairness to his two sisters, was later deducted from his inheritance—he bought gold shares and invested in businesses of a new mining town, Carletonville, that mushroomed on the barren African veldt.

By 1943 he laid out the township of Oberholzer close to a railway line that bordered our farm, naming the streets after his family, like Ida Street, and the Dutch Royal family. He sat on many committees, and was the only farmer in the Rotary Club. He had made a name for himself.

During the war years the only contact my father had with his family was a single page, censored letter, once a month. A telegram announcing the birth of my brother in 1940 got lost in the turmoil that followed Germany's invasion of the Netherlands.

In late 1947, my father decided to take us to the Netherlands to meet his parents and other family. My mother was ecstatic: this was her chance to get a new wardrobe for herself and my brother and me. My brother and I were happy; we didn't have to go to school for three months.

A while before our departure we gathered in the living room for our usual afternoon tea. My father, sitting in his favorite chair, closed a large book as we walked in.

Looking smug he said, "Well my children,"—this included my mother—"I have some news." He had just discovered that his family name Hommes originated from that of a noble family dating back to the 16th century. "From now on," he said, nobly waving his hand, "whenever you come into my presence, you have to bow down and address me as Lord."

My mother said, "Hah, forget it!"

My brother and I, impressed with our father's elevated status, played along. For the next few days we bowed and scraped and addressed our father as "Lord Pappa." All in fun.

[Many years after my father's death in 1978, my mother handed me a book that traced her ancestors back to 1640. It inspired me to research our family's genealogical background, including tracking that noble family my father bragged about. Who knows, I might have a legitimate claim to a castle somewhere.

But it was not to be. What I did find was that our family name, and that of all Groningers dated back only to 1812. Before that it was the custom to give children their father's first name as a family name.

An example: my ancestor, Onno Bartelds married Elizabeth Geerts in 1698.

They had eight children. One son was named Geert Onnes. (His mother's last name and his father's first name. Onno became Onnes.)

Geert Onnes married Vaya Renken in1730. They had nine children who all got the family name of Geerts. Each child of Onno Bartelds and Elizabeth Geerts carried their name over to their own children, with the result that in one family of eight children, there was a tangled web of family names.

Napoleon put a stop to all that. During the years 1795 to 1812, when the Netherlands was part of the French empire, new laws were imposed on the Dutch. One of them: by 1812 each family had to choose a permanent family name. My father's family chose the name Hommes and my mother's family the name Engels.

And that noble family? No trace anywhere. I discovered instead that my father descended from a long line—dating back six centuries—of hardworking farmers and that his great-grand father was a simple farmhand who had the good fortune to catch the eye of the only daughter of a well-to-do farmer.]

We sailed for the Netherlands in late March 1948, our family car, a bright green Nash, 1947 model, in the hold of the ship. At Rotterdam harbor our family greeted us in typical Dutch fashion: friendly, low key, no hugs, and a great deal of curiosity. Along the road to Groningen, we passed miles of tulip fields in full bloom, and skeletal remains of bombed out buildings. Everything clean and tidy. We stayed with my grandparents who lived on a tree lined street in a charming rural town, with a single windmill surrounded by farmlands.

If my parents were aware of the still dire living conditions in the Netherlands, they didn't tell us. There was a shortage of food and other commodities. Our family used precious coupons to put better food—like white bread—on the table for us. Transportation was limited; most people didn't own a car. But we did. We

Travelling Beyond Borders

drove around in our big car, feeling very important, especially on Sundays when driving was restricted to emergency vehicles, the police and foreign visitors.

While we swanked around in our new wardrobes, most people wore old, sometimes mended clothes, and patched up shoes. I met a younger cousin who wore an old dress of mine and shoes I had outgrown.

Our ostentation did not sit well with some of our family. One uncle, with thinly veiled sarcasm, addressed my father as the Baron of Oberholzer. What others thought of us, I don't know.

On a balmy spring day when we were on our way to visit family in a nearby town, my mother came downstairs carrying a silver fox fur jacket.

My grandmother took one look at it and said, "The only women who wear that kind of thing these days are the prostitutes who sold themselves to Nazi occupiers."

Wham! My mother, furious, ran upstairs, dumped the fur jacket, and stalked out of the house in high dudgeon.

For the next few days my mother sulked, and whenever my mother sulked life for the rest of us became downright unpleasant. My father in some desperation arranged for my other grandmother—who was also visiting her family—to take care of my brother and me. While we stayed in a small hotel at a vacation resort in a forest, he took my mother—and her fur jacket—on a three week tour of Switzerland, Italy and Spain.

Our three month visit finally came to an end, and we were ready to go home again. Relations between my mother and her mother-in-law remained strained, but polite. On the whole it was a good visit and we came away with many fond memories.

We flew back home on a small airplane that only carried about forty passengers. It functioned more like an air bus, with frequent landings to refuel, give passengers a chance to use the toilet and get something to eat.

From Europe we flew to the French Colony of Algeria and landed at the

Algiers airport late one afternoon to have dinner and use the toilet. As we walked in something caught my attention.

In a loud excited voice I said, "Pappa, look!"

Bystanders looked in the direction I pointed, my mother started to laugh and my father's face turned red. There, on the door of the men's toilet, in big bold letters, was our family name: HOMMES.

A Pioneer in Africa

In his book: *Lost Trails of the Transvaal*, T.V. Bulpin wrote:

The infinite patience and artistry of that old craftsman, Nature, have wrought upon the face of earth some wondrous scenes and changes. With the irresistible erosion of the elements as the principal tool, all manner of strange shapes have been ingeniously contrived. Deserts and mountains and oceans have been made, and then, through some whim, the whole lot changed; the plateaux into seas; the seas into deserts; and some long-standing geological system of a magnitude staggering to mankind simply vanished away as easily as a misspelt word is changed in a schoolchild's lesson book.

That segment of the complex face of Africa . . . called the Transvaal, has known in full measure the sublime cycle of restless creation . . . there is no section possessing a greater variety of scenic marvels, a more complex geological history, or a richer endowment bequeathed to it from the mineral treasure chest of providence.

The [Western] Transvaal is . . . a spacious and temperate grassland, almost devoid of trees, well-watered, green and sun drenched in summer; dry, brown and crisply cold in winter . . . .

But it is beneath the surface of this majestic and varied land that its most potent magic lies. Nearly every precious stone, mineral and metal known to man has been found there in deposits varying from traces to quantities of enormous value, has been found there. Antimony, arsenic, asbestos, chromium coal, cobalt, copper, corundum, diamonds, gemstones, gold, iron, lead, limestone, salt, manganese, marble, mica, nickel, oil shale, platinum, silver, tantalum, tin tungsten, vanadium—to name only a few, have all been discovered in the Transvaal by the enterprise of countless eager prospectors.

In a letter my father wrote to his parents in Holland in December 1947, he recalled his first journey through South Africa in 1928: *"It is now 19 years ago that I passed here by train from Cape Town to Johannesburg, without knowing that I would spend so many years of my life here. I remember so well how often I asked myself on that long 1600 kilometer train journey where I would end up in this vast country, and what the future would hold for me."*

My father's first view of the desolate place where he was to settle as a farmer did not impress him very much. There was no platform where the train briefly stopped. A painted sign with "Oberholzer" perching precariously on the roof of a corrugated iron shack, acted as a beacon that there were people somewhere eking out a living on the land. A dirt road, not clearly defined, sloped down to a shallow valley about a mile away, and then upward again to disappear in the far distant horizon. In the valley stood a few indigenous trees, randomly planted by nature, and fed with water from an underground spring.

On the other side of the train tracks, close by, stood a lonely little house sheltered by a single tree. Who lived there? Farther on, a vast treeless veldt undulated towards a range of boulder covered hills in the distance, all covered with dusty dull summer green. No sign of life anywhere.

With the keen eyes of a budding farmer, my father decided then and there that this was useless as potential farmland.

But several months later there he was getting off the train where the name Oberholzer still perched on the corrugated shed. A strip of land that stretched from the train tracks down to the valley where water bubbled out of the earth was now his. He was twenty-two years old, and a pioneer farmer.

The first years were difficult. He lived in a two-room, two-window mud hut, no running water, and an outhouse in the back. In the room that functioned as kitchen, a-beer-saturated black man, named Cigarette, cooked barely edible food on a primus stove till his future mother-in-law, on a neighboring farm, rescued him with an invitation for daily dinner.

Travelling Beyond Borders

He discovered that the rock strewn veldt did not end on the other side of the rail tracks: the ox-pulled plough working his land churned up rocks, big and small before the earth was ready for planting.

Generous rain showers and benevolent sun made the wheat grow lush until, once, a dark cloud rained locusts from the sky and destroyed it all in a matter of minutes; or a freak fifteen minute hailstorm flattened rows of straight-growing corn.

His herd of dairy cows delivered ample milk, till mastitis (a strep infection of the udder) wreaked havoc, forcing him to sell them at a pittance to be slaughtered for meat.

Barclay's Bank refused to loan him money to buy more healthy cows: *not before you have a thousand pounds in your account, Mister Hommes.* His father sent money with a note: *consider this your inheritance.*

There were times when all the disasters and lack of money brought him to the brink of despair. But the future was not entirely bleak. Eight years after he started farming, he married the young woman from the neighboring farm in 1934, and two years later had a baby daughter.

Then stunning news. Those boulder strewn hills and barren veldt he had written off years ago as useless farmland had for thousands of years concealed deep underground an immense treasure: gold!

My father knew then why Providence had planted him on this spot in Africa. It was Opportunity, and he grabbed it with both hands. A pioneer farmer turned into businessman and community developer. His life would never be the same.

"What's in a Name?"
A Story of Two Grandmothers

It was the name my parents chose for me that triggered the rift between my two grandmothers. My maternal grandmother, Grietje Engels, lived on a farm in South Africa about two miles from ours. My other grandmother, also named Grietje or "Oma Holland" as we later called her—lived in the Province of Groningen, Holland, where both my parents were born.

I was the first grandchild and my anticipated arrival caused great excitement in both families. The telegram announcing my birth to my grandparents in Holland, however, was met with some disappointment. It read: *It's a girl. Name: Grietje.*

A telegram of congratulations was soon followed by a blunt letter from my grandmother. She wrote in the typical staccato style in which she also spoke the Groninger dialect: *So it's a girl? I know you wanted a son. Better luck next time. Why do you want to name her Grietje? It's an ugly name! I don't like it! Choose another name!*

The letter stunned my parents. They had hoped in this way to honor both grandmothers, and avoid hurt feelings, since both were named Grietje. They could not figure out the reason behind this nasty letter. After some thought, my grandfather Engels suggested naming me Ida, after his elder sister who was only eighteen years old when she died in 1897. A safe bet that no one would be made happy or unhappy with this choice.

My two grandmothers met for the first time when Grietje and Eggo Hommes came to South Africa in 1936 to meet their six-month-old granddaughter and to check on the progress of their son's farm, which they bought him in 1928.

Travelling Beyond Borders

It soon became clear that the name Grietje was all my grandmothers shared. For the rest, no two women could be further apart in appearance and character. Grietje Engels, her beautiful face framed with thick naturally curly hair, had large hazel eyes and a full mouth that radiated warmth and gentility. She never, in all the years I knew her, raised her voice in anger or frustration.

In contrast, Grietje Hommes had thin straight hair kept in a tight bun, small eyes and pouting mouth. Her demeanor was that of a strong, no nonsense woman who spoke in a staccato voice which increased in sharpness as she grew older. There was nothing soft about her. Any feelings of emotion or affection were hidden behind a brusque manner. Instead of a kiss and hug, her children and grandchildren were greeted with a handshake.

Although I was pronounced to be "an adorable baby" the visit did not heal the rift that the nasty letter started. But the farm! Grietje declared it, "A mess!"

She did not take into account that farming in South Africa was different than in Groningen and that fickle Mother Nature had played a role too. In the first years my father had difficulty communicating his instructions to the black laborers who did not understand Dutch and he did not know their language, Sesotho, with the result that things were often done wrong or not all. On the dairy farm the spreading of infectious mastitis (a strep infection of the udder) had wreaked havoc among the milk producing cows, forcing my father to sell them at a pittance for slaughter. Spells of draught had killed tender crops. And plowing large tracts of land with a team of oxen took longer than a tractor, slowing the planting process.

"Buy him a tractor," she told my grandfather, "and healthy cows." He did.

My mother's housekeeping was also carefully scrutinized and pronounced okay—since the black maids were doing all the hard work of cleaning the house, gathering the eggs, and peeling the potatoes. But—she could not resist saying—my mother did not know how to make good butter and probably never would.

This did not sit well with Grietje Engels. In a calm voice laced with gentle irony she told Grietje Hommes that my mother had learned to milk a cow, (which Grietje Hommes did not) and all about making butter, how to work a butter churn, since her teenage years; and how to turn every part of a slaughtered pig into something edible. And she was proud that her three daughters had, with her guidance, turned out to be good housewives.

None of this had any effect on Grietje Hommes. She returned to Holland, satisfied that she had set everything and everybody straight, totally unaware that her tactless manner had spoiled all possibilities of conciliation between the two families.

Two years later, 1938, another daughter was born. My parents, forewarned, named her Ada Elizabeth, after a close friend. To their surprise another blunt letter followed the telegram from Holland. This time my grandmother expressed her hurt and outrage that the second daughter was not named after her!

"Aha," said my grandfather Engels, "It is now very clear why Grietje Hommes objected to the name the first time around: jealousy of Grietje Engels." He wrote a letter to the Hommes grandparents and did not mince words. Instead of addressing them directly he began his letter with "What's in a Name?" in English then wrote the rest of the letter in Dutch:

Two years ago, he wrote, *you considered the name Grietje odious. The poor child would be stuck with a name she would probably hate, you said. Now with Baby #2 the name suddenly seems very acceptable. We don't know how to understand this other than that in your misguided jealousy you manipulated all of us into choosing another name and thereby deprive my Grietje the honor of having a child named after her.* No reply came from Holland. My parents, in an attempt to smooth hurt feelings named their second daughter, Greta—a nicer version of Grietje. The rift remained. (My little sister Greta died of convulsions when she was eighteen months old. When my daughter was born, I named her Greta in memory of my sister. My parents were moved and happy.)

Many years later Grietje Hommes proved to be right in one instance: two of my cousins, one named after Grietje Engels, the other after Grietje Hommes, declared they hated the name. After our beloved grandmother Engels died in 1957 my cousin Grietje Hiemstra officially changed her name to Gretchen, the German version of Grietje. The other granddaughter in Holland, Grietje de Jong, changed the spelling—and the pronunciation—to Greetje, after she saw a photo in a Groninger newspaper of a champion milk producing cow, named Grietje!

NOTES:

1. This story was based on copies of letters from my father; my grandfather Engels (from whom I got the title "What's in a Name"); a copy of a letter my grandmother Hommes sent to an Agricultural organization in Groningen who were interested in farming in South Africa, particularly the situation of my father's farm in 1936; stories my mother told me; and my own experience with both grandmothers.

2. I was already an adult when my mother told me about the childhood of my grandmother Grietje Hommes, which might explain why she was as stand-offish and remote as an adult.

She was the only child of a rather well to do farmer. Her mother died when she was about two years old. Soon after, he married another woman to take care of the house and his daughter. This woman turned out to be a mean stepmother, often punishing little Grietje without reason. For instance, instead of a gift at Christmas she got a little bag of salt because she was "a bad girl." Her father didn't care for her because she was "just a girl." The result was that Grietje grew up in a lonely loveless environment which affected her outlook on life. She didn't know how to communicate with people other than in a tactless way and because she trusted no-one. Until she met my grandfather: he was a kind, caring benevolent man with an astute business sense. I don't know what he saw in her, but she was not as dour as she often appeared; she could be friendly and laugh at a good joke so when he proposed in 1903, she accepted him.

When Grietje's father died she inherited his entire estate; a farm with a two story house and money in the bank. This was an ample dowry to bring into a marriage. My grandfather sold the farm and invested the money in Dutch stocks and shares that grew in value through the years, which enabled him to create a trust fund that would support my grandmother after his death in 1950. She died in 1966.

The Station Master's Wife

There wasn't even a platform to set foot on when the Engels family arrived at their destination. A corrugated iron shack with a place name "Oberholzer" on the roof, passed for a train station. Across the train tracks, sheltered by a few Eucalyptus trees, stood a small house with an open porch. Sitting on a bench with one leg comfortably folded under her bulk, was a very fat woman: the only sign of life in the quiet that settled after the train had left. That was Tannie Kok, the station master's wife. In her hand, a leg of lamb from which she pulled the last bits of meat with her teeth while waving a cheery hello and welcome to the stunned family.

Tannie Kok was a typical Afrikaner woman: jovial and kind with a wonderful sense for comic drama. Her husband, Oom Kok, was shorter and two sizes smaller. "Circle and Dot" (O .) people called them. That's the way it looked when they drove up on their horse and buggy three days later to visit the Engels family: Tannie Kok taking up most of the narrow seat while Oom Kok sitting precariously close to the edge, held the reins in one hand and the other on the handrail to keep from falling off.

She brought a milk tart, Tannie Kok said, to introduce a Dutch family to a favorite Afrikaner dessert. She was curious too she admitted, to see "how you foreigners are settling down in your new country," amused by their attempts to speak Afrikaans.

My grandmother complained about all the dirt she found in the old, neglected farmhouse the first time she walked in: the thick layer of red dust that covered everything, cockroaches running about and finding mice droppings in the pantry. There was no bathroom. Worst of all, no toilet, only a smelly outhouse standing in a patch of overgrown weeds where one of the boys discovered a large snake.

Tannie Kok had advice for almost everything: get two black women from the native compound to come sweep and clean. For roaches and mice, the strong smell of Khaki bushes (in the Marigold family) placed around the house, and in the attic, would get rid of them in no time. As for using the outhouse at night, "Put some piss pots under the beds," she said with a loud laugh. "We all do."

And, just as she told everyone in the farming community, *She* was actually the Station Master, her husband was only the "Master of Loading and Unloading." As usual Oom Kok took all his wife's ribbing with good humor and a shy smile.

There was only one time that Oom Kok's good humor failed him: when an irate farmer threatened to beat him up. Something had gone wrong with goods that were not properly delivered and the farmer blamed Oom Kok for the mishap.

Tannie Kok sitting in her favorite place on the porch watched while the farmer—towering over her husband—yelled profanities at him. It was too much for her.

With remarkable agility she walked over to the two men, pushed her husband aside, saying, "Stand over there, you'll get hurt," and planted her full weight in front of the farmer and with hands akimbo said, "What's your problem?"

The startled farmer mumbled something, turned around and left.

Tannie Kok made full use of her title as Station Master. Whenever she went shopping at the nearest town, fifteen miles away, she took the train. It was an entertaining spectacle for the few who happened to be at the train stop on that day. Oom Kok, waved a white flag at the approaching train—the only way to signal STOP—then helped hoist his wife's 300-pound freight into a chair on the balcony of the caboose. When she was comfortably settled with a food basket on her lap, he waved the flag again and off the train went. Tannie Kok seated on her private balcony, waved goodbye like the Queen of England as the train disappeared in the distance.

NOTE:

In 1928 my grandparents, Engel and Grietje Engels plus their six children (ages four to fifteen) went to South Africa to settle as pioneer Dutch farmers in the spacious veldt of the Western Transvaal in a place called Oberholzer.

Adult Afrikaner women were traditionally called "Tannie" (Aunty).

Adult Afrikaner men "Oom" (Uncle).

Section II: Childhood on the Farm

A New Country

Guardian Angel

A Day on a South African Farm

Saara's Story

Little Buck

Medicine Woman

The End of an Affair

Getting Religion

A New Country

Once Africa grabs hold of your heart strings, it pulls hard and never lets go. Africa stuns your senses with its pulsating life; in the rhythmic heartbeat de-dum-te-dum of drums that fills the night air; the ways of its people; the infinite variety of animals roaming free in the wilderness; soaring mountains; verdant forests; unique flora; the vast veldt that stretches to the edge of the world; the golden sun; and the busy noise of its cities and the sudden stillness that announces the end of another day on a farm. There is no other place like it in the world.

I was born on that farm where the sudden stillness announced the end of another day. Where the veldt beyond our farm stretched to the edge of the world, there where the golden sun went down to make way for the moon and the Milky Way, and the rhythmic heartbeat sound of African drums lulled me to sleep.

The sounds of farm life became as familiar to me as my mother's voice while I was still in my crib. As a toddler I began to distinguish the nuances of five different languages: the Groninger dialect, Dutch, English, Afrikaans, and the unique lilt of Sesotho. By the time I went to school I could more or less speak them all.

Each language represented a different cultural group, all clustered together in a place called Oberholzer. As a child my daily encounter with the people of these various cultures left several distinct impressions on me.

There was the immediate Dutch/Groninger farmer community of my parents and grandparents. We followed Dutch customs: celebrating New Years day with traditional *Oliebollen* (deep fried raisin filled dough balls sprinkled with powdered sugar). We ate food prepared the Dutch way: Saturday dinner was always pea soup with slices of spicy sausage and chunks of potato, followed by thick pan sized pancakes spread with homemade butter and brown sugar, or my favorite buttermilk and barley soup sweetened with a few spoons of Lyle's Golden syrup.

The English, who moved into the Oberholzer area after gold was discovered around 1937 five miles away, were the true colonials, drank whiskey at sundown and ate kippers for breakfast. They were the doctors, lawyers and business developers of the new mining town, Carletonville, that mushroomed on the barren South African veldt.

The religiously conservative Afrikaners, who considered alcohol and dancing—of unmarried body-touching couples—a sin that led to all sorts of sexual mischief, despised the English for invading their country and winning the Anglo-Boer war. They were the poor struggling farmers, train conductors, postmen, policemen, and drove the busses.

The blacks, fenced in like cattle by the laws of Apartheid, tilled the land, milked the cows, and cleaned the houses of the whites. They sang and danced to the beat of drums in communication with the spirits of their ancestors while offering thanks for the *Kaffir* beer they drank. Their staple food of *Putu* (thickened cornmeal porridge; pronounced pootoo) was augmented with cooked *Morogo* (field spinach). Occasionally a snake roasted over a wood fire, and peeled prickly pears for dessert. Other times, when a cloud of locusts rained from the sky to wreak havoc on the crops of the white farmers, the black women and children gleefully ran to the land, gathered them in any container they could find, threw them into the cooking pot and had a feast. Or in early spring when fat green Mopane worms—*Nottos* in Sesotho—fell to the ground gorged with the blossoms of Acacia trees, everyone snacked on cooked protein rich sun-dried Nottos.

A few Indian families living on my father's farm added variety to the cultural mix. The men were the shopkeepers. The women wore bright colorful saris, chewed betel nuts (a stimulant drug), and served curried food to their families three times a day.

With so many different cultures living together in the ever expanding community of Oberholzer it was inevitable that some customs and tastes would spill over into another group. The Dutch took to drinking sundowners like the English.

Travelling Beyond Borders

Both the English and Dutch took to the Afrikaner *braaivleis* (barbeque), relishing a meal of *Boerewors* (homemade farmer-sausage) and Putu, something unheard of in a Dutch house or in Mother Country, England. And everyone happily added Indian curry dishes to their menus.

But how did a group of Dutch people from the Province of Groningen in the Netherlands come to settle in Oberholzer in a remote corner of the Western Transvaal in the first place?

It all began when a cocky little fellow named Napoleon hoisted his five foot six frame onto a mighty stallion, waved his sword in the air and shouted, "Follow me men, I'm going to conquer Russia!"

That was in 1812. By then France had already governed the Netherlands for about seventeen years. From 1795 to 1813 the Netherlands formed part of the French empire. It was not an entirely hostile occupation since a great many Dutch anti-monarchists had invited the French to rescue them from the so-called dictatorship of the Dutch king. They deposed the king, and the Netherlands became the Republic of Batavia, with French and Dutch as the official languages and French laws founded on Liberty, Equality, Fraternity, were put into place.

All of which gave Napoleon leave to conscript over a thousand Dutch men into his army and, as one historian put it, using the Netherlands as "a generous milking cow," milking the country dry of all its resources to feed his army.

In the end it was all for nothing. Napoleon lost the battle. Hiding in a closed coach he scurried back to Paris to lick his wounds, leaving behind close to 400,000 dead or dying soldiers—and his mighty stallion—to rot on the snow covered Steppes of Russia. (Russian composer Pyotr Tchaikovsky composed the "1812 Overture" in 1880 to commemorate the Russian victory over Napoleon in 1812.)

Meanwhile the Dutch people decided they had had enough of French governance. It had been a big mistake, they realized, to depose their monarch. They begged him to come back and occupy the throne again, which he graciously consented to do.

But all was not well in the Netherlands. The Dutch economy was in shambles. Farmers, robbed of the horses that pulled the plows to plant crops to feed their cattle that provided milk and meat to the population, struggled to get back on their feet. The result was a severe food shortage, especially from 1823 to 1837.

Just when it all seemed hopeless, Providence came to the rescue.

It's a story that goes back to when Mother Nature was still shaping the face of the earth and used that part of the world known as the Netherlands—the flat land-below-sea-level—as a sort of testing area for natural disasters, in particular the Province of Groningen. With mischievous glee she generated hurricanes, churned up the North Sea, then dumped the whole lot on the defenseless low lying land, causing floods and destruction of almost all that lived and grew there. With no mountains or hills to protect them from floods, the resilient survivors built higher and higher dykes, planted crops, built houses and communities, again and again.

Mother Nature, however, was not always bent on death and destruction, she could also be benevolent. Through the centuries the repeated flooding dumped rich layers of silt called "sea clay" containing magnesium, calcium (all those ground up seashells), and a lot of other minerals that made it ideal for planting wheat and other crops. The richest layer of sea clay was deposited in the north-eastern part of Groningen where my parents were born.

The farmers there, unaware of this gift from the sea, concentrated on dairy farming and the crops they planted used mainly to feed cattle. Then another disaster hit: a virus that caused an incurable disease, Rinderpest, killed most of the cattle and decimated the dairy industry. By the end of the 18th century, most farmers had given up on dairy farming and started cultivating food crops. The time, the place, soil conditions, all played a role in creating what became known as an agricultural phenomenon in Groningen.

Travelling Beyond Borders

From about 1835 to 1877 top quality grains at premium prices poured across Groningen's borders into all corners of Western Europe, and tons of money poured right back into the coffers of a majority of Groninger farmers, among them my two great-great grandfathers. All this money meant a big step up on the social ladder: they were no longer mere farmers but Gentleman Farmers, a title they proudly flaunted by replacing their small farmhouses with two or three story mansions, furnished with elegant furniture and oriental carpets.

Instead of shoveling manure, the farmers joined book clubs, smoked expensive cigars, meddled in local politics, and chose the pastors of their community church. Their wives no longer milked the cows but employed maids to do the dirty work. Their children no longer helped out on the farm but instead were sent to finishing schools in foreign countries like Germany, Austria, and France.

By 1877 the grain producing boom in Groningen had reached its peak. Signs that the good times were coming to an end loomed on the horizon: steamships loaded with much cheaper grains from the American Midwest sailed en masse towards the shores of Europe and by 1895 had taken over the territorial Groninger market.

America not only produced cheaper grains, it revolutionized farming techniques: steel plows replaced wooden plows, followed later by the tractor and steam operated threshing machines replaced field hands.

Groningen farmers fought a losing battle, not only in competing with the cheaper grains, but through lack of space: the entire Province of Groningen would probably fit onto a single wheat producing farm in the Midwest. All this effectively changed the agricultural industry of Groningen and significantly the fortunes of many farmers, including my father, the only son, due to inherit the family farm.

When he turned eighteen in 1924, my father, with the same astute business sense as his father, told his parents that farming in Groningen was no longer lucrative and that it would be better if he moved to another country, like South

Africa, to seek his fortunes. His parents agreed and offered to advance him his inheritance to buy land and everything else needed to create a lucrative farm.

He arrived in South Africa on December 23rd, 1928. Eight months later he bought the farm in Oberholzer and with other Dutch settlers, like my fourteen-year-old mother and her family who also arrived there in 1928, established the community in which I grew up.

My roots are firmly embedded in the Groninger soil where my ancestors, farmers all, tilled the land since the 15th century. But thanks in part to those clever Mid-West Americans, I was the first Groninger child in our family destined to be born in a new country, South Africa.

My childhood memories border on the idyllic, but I cannot deny or forget the evils of Apartheid that permeated all of our lives. I was a privileged white child and did not suffer under it. But my nanny, Lisa, who taught me her lilting language, Sesotho, did. So did Saara our black housemaid, who guided me through tribal lore and customs and who gifted me with jubilant song and the Sotho tribal dance of wedding celebration on my wedding day. It was they and the ways of their people who grabbed hold of my heartstrings that keeps pulling me back to Africa and a memorable childhood.

Guardian Angel

One source defines a guardian angel this way:
Your Guardian Angel has been with you since you took your first breath and will be there for you when you pass out of your body and return to the spiritual realms. This Angel is unique to you and will walk with you wherever you go and whatever you do. You are never alone!

When I was a child the expression "guardian angel" always conjured up a vision of some winged being dressed in white that floated a few feet above your head. It was something like the angel who delivered the baby of our black maid Saara, as she told five-year-old me, and left in the ruins of a mud hut on the South African veldt just beyond our farm. Only, a guardian angel was always there, while Saara's angel flew back to heaven in the white airplane that God used for such purposes and kept anchored on a cloud when not in use, which was seldom.

As a child I had no use for a guardian angel; I was too busy with growing up and discovering life. It was only as an adult when I realized that from the day I was born, and later whenever I encountered an obstacle or some emotional conflict, my Oma (grandmother) Grietje Engels had quietly played the role of guardian angel and supported me in some way or other. I was her first grand-child.

A late March thunderstorm was raging outside the hospital window in 1936 while my mother struggled to push me out of her womb and the good doctor finally took matters in hand and pulled me out with forceps. "It's a girl!" he exclaimed as the nurse whisked me out of the room.

Oma wrote a letter to my mother the next day to tell her what happened next:
Jan and I were getting worried about how long it took for you to deliver your baby when the nurse, red in the face, suddenly walked into the waiting room, put your

unwashed, wrapped in a towel baby on my lap and to our surprise stalked out without a word. We didn't know if it was a girl or boy so we took a peek. "What a small ugly thing she is," Jan said. He was a bit disappointed that it wasn't the son he expected, but he was very happy that it turned out well and that your baby seems healthy . . .

That's how my Oma, and not my mother, was the first one to hold me and whisper, "*Welkom mien lutje wicht,*" (welcome my little girl) in her Groninger dialect.

In the rest of her letter she wrote, *Your little girl*—I had no name yet—*will soon grow fat with mother's milk and in a short while the dents on her skull from the forceps will be gone. I promise she will be a joy to you and Jan.*

She also wrote about her conversation with my father during the 25 mile drive on the rain soaked dirt road back to the farm. She told him the same thing and consoled him with the thought that the next baby might be a son, and that they celebrated my birth with a hefty glass of red wine.

She was right. In less than three months I was no longer scrawny or ugly and my father wrote to his parents in Holland expressing his pride; *She is beautiful, makes a lot of noise, is demanding and has the same healthy appetite as the calves on the farm.*

Four years later my father's wish for a son was answered. The joyful news of my brother's birth in June 1940, however, was bracketed with tragedy and grief.

In May came the news of Nazi Germany's invasion of Holland, followed soon after by the devastating news of the death of Oma's younger sister—married to a physician—who took her own life when the German tanks rumbled past their house.

Holland was in chaos. Letters and news to the outside world were restricted and censored, increasing the worries of what further disaster might lie ahead for the Dutch people and their beloved country.

A telegram to announce my brother's birth took almost a month to get through the censors before it reached my father's parents. Another telegram to announce the birth of his first great-grandson reached the ninety-year-old patriarch of the Engels family just a few days before he died on July 15th.

Oma remembered her tough, no nonsense father-in-law with gratitude: from the gold bracelet he gave her as a wedding gift in 1912, and passing the family farm on to them; a generous gift that enabled Opa (my grandfather) to sell it and use the money to buy a farm in South Africa in 1928 when a doctor recommended that a warmer drier climate would be beneficial.

Then another blow struck. On the 12th of October my 53-year-old Opa, who was slowly recuperating from yet another illness—in the same hospital where I was born—suddenly collapsed and died on his way to the toilet.

Oma was only 51 years old but decided that with the help of her three sons she could still run the farm successfully. That lasted only a year. Her oldest son was not interested in farming and moved out. The second son had brains enough to keep the books, but suffered from epileptic seizures, which made any manual work like driving a tractor a dangerous prospect. That left her with her sixteen-year-old son, Eltjo, more inclined to fooling around with the black farmhands—who fondly called him "Mafuta" (the chubby one)—than supervising them, and little sense of the responsibility of running a farm.

So Oma bravely soldiered on with what she had, while my brother and I grew up. Our parents got more involved with social events on the gold mining town five miles away from our farm and we got to spend the weekend with Oma. We loved to visit there, getting to do things we never did on our own farm.

At Oma's house there were no toys. She didn't read to us or tell bedtime stories. Instead, we lived the stories. We fed the clucking hens in the cozy chicken coop; picked our own eggs from their nests—"I want *this* one, Oma"—for breakfast; and felt the velvety down of newly hatched chicks in our hands and mimicked their "peep-peep," while Oma watched as we carefully put them down close to the feeder. In the stable she guided our small hands as we awkwardly tugged the teats of the cows to make the milk come out. I didn't like touching the cow teats, "I'm scared . . ." I wailed. Oma said it was okay.

On other visits we helped her stir the butter churn; picked our own corn or strawberries in the vegetable garden for our supper; helped gather quinces in the orchard to make jelly, or apples to make apple sauce; and holding her hand tightly, watched, fascinated, how the bees buzzed in from the Alfalfa fields and deposited the precious nectar inside the three beehives that stood in a neat row along the orchard fence.

"See, they're making honey," Oma would whisper. "You have to be very quiet and not disturb them, otherwise they will sting you."

We knew from experience that a bee sting was painful so whenever we visited the beehives, we stood at a safe distance and kept still.

Saturday night was bath night at Oma's house. It wasn't always a pleasant experience for us. Oma was a firm believer in washing in tepid water no matter the season.

"It's good for the circulation," she would say. Only cold water, pumped up by the creaking windmill from deep underground, flowed out of the tap into the cement tub. With no water heater, two large kettles of boiling water from the wood burning stove in the kitchen had to do the job.

Once in the tub, Oma would alternately scrub us clean with her homemade soap, dry our shivering bodies with a rough sun dried towel till our skins glowed, then help us into our pajamas and thick hand knitted wool socks. We went through this little ordeal without complaint because there was always the promise of a slice of white bread, smeared thickly with homemade butter and sprinkled with sugar for supper. But before that we had to eat a slice of dense rye bread (pumpernickel)—spread with honey—that she had baked in round coffee tins. "It makes you poop," she would say with a sly smile, knowing we would laugh that she had said a "bad" word.

I always enjoyed those evenings when it was just the three of us at the supper table, lit by a petroleum lamp that enclosed us in cozy dome of light. Our uncle Eltjo, who lived in a rondawel (round house) next to Oma's house, was usually out with his friend Henry to a dance or a beer party at the mine town five miles away.

The first time I became aware that Oma was playing the role of guardian angel was when I was about five and she came to drink tea with us one day.

I showed her my doll and said, "My baby is sick. I want to be a nurse when I grow up so that I can make my baby better."

My mother let out a loud laugh and said sarcastically, "You, a nurse? How can you be a nurse if you vomit or faint every time I take you to the hospital for your shots?" Which was true.

It must have been the hurt look on my face that prompted Oma to come to the rescue. She recognized my symptoms: our shared interest in anything medical and caring for the sick.

She quietly took me by the hand and in her calm soothing voice said, "Come, I'll show you how to make little pills that will make sick people better."

In the kitchen she mixed a bit of flour with water and showed me how to roll the thick paste into little pills and put them in a neat row on a cookie sheet.

"Now we're going to put them in the sun to dry."

"But I want to look like the nurses in the hospital when I give people pills," I said.

"We can fix that too," she replied. We went to the bedroom, found an old cloth diaper of my baby brother, and pinned it around my head to look like a veil.

I didn't tell Oma that no one, not even the dog, wanted to take my sun dried, fly inspected pills, except my father who gamely swallowed two and said it made him feel much better. She would have been very disappointed, I thought, so I stopped playing nurse for the time being. Soon after, a new adventure loomed on the horizon: school, and a new interest: reading.

I was ten years old when Oma suffered another blow that affected all of us.

Everyone was stunned by the news that my gentle, kind 22-year-old uncle Eltjo had been arrested with his friend Henry for the murder of an old black man.

I picked up most of the story from my mother who gave vent to her emotions with angry rants against everyone involved: the police, the judge, even Eltjo's friend Henry. It was everybody's fault except her little brother's, who was innocent!

The real story was this: late one night on their way home from a beer party they saw an old black man riding his bike in the middle of the dirt road who, as they testified in court, did not get out of the way when the truck came closer.

It must have been a blend of too much beer and an excess of testosterone that made them stop the truck, knock the defenseless old man off his bike, beat him up "to teach him a lesson," and leave him lying beside of the road, and drive off.

Three weeks later the old man died of bleeding on the brain. He had managed to get home after he regained consciousness and told his family that he recognized Henry, a mechanic who worked in the local garage, as one of the men who beat him. After his death his family contacted the police and told them what happened. A court case followed and based on all the circumstantial evidence; the judge sentenced both men to six months in a minimum security jail.

My mother was outraged. She condemned the judge to hell and found no consolation in my father's sober words, "They can be damn lucky that it is just six months. It could have been three to five years in a maximum security jail." And never, throughout the whole drama, do I remember hearing a single word of sympathy from anyone for the black man's family who had lost a husband and father.

The prisoners were allowed family visits once a month. I begged my mother to let me go along on the first visit. Oma said it was okay.

I have only a few vivid memories of that day so long ago: my mother driving the car, Oma next to her nervously dabbing her face with a white handkerchief, me sitting on the back seat wondering about the jail and Uncle Eltjo. Would we see him handcuffed and his legs in chains? Would he be upset? Or cry?

If it were not for the ten feet high wire fence that surrounded the jail complex, visitors could have mistaken it for a small vegetable farm situated in peaceful countryside surrounded by low shrub-covered hills in the distance.

At the gate a guard promptly confiscated the cookies Oma brought then told us to wait, while another guard called for "Prisoner Engels." Uncle Eltjo dressed in plain khaki pants and shirt—and unshackled—was happy to see us.

We sat on wood benches under a shady tree and he told us about life in prison. All the prisoners took turns working in the vegetable gardens, planting, and weeding, cleaning their cells, doing laundry and keeping the complex in pristine condition. After an hour we had to leave. Oma was clearly relieved that Uncle Eltjo seemed to be doing okay in prison. Six months later he was back on the farm, and life went on.

My life changed when I turned 13. I was sent to a boarding school in Pretoria and for the next five years saw less of Oma or spent the night with her again. Those days were over. After graduating high school, I went to the University of Pretoria then on to nursing school. It made her very happy, Oma told me, that my childhood dream had become reality.

It was at the University that I met my future husband, Hendrik, a theology student working on his master's degree in philosophy. My choice of husband did not go over well with my parents. My father was somewhat skeptical about my life as the wife of a pastor, but if that was what I wanted, then so be it. My mother's vehement, bordering on vicious comments pained me very much. Everything counted against him. He was an Afrikaner; she didn't like Afrikaners. He was short, not handsome, an unromantic intellectual. How could I ever be happy with such a man? Oma, on the other hand, welcomed Hendrik with friendly warmth. She saw the man I saw: kind, caring and solid.

"I like him very much and I know you will be happy with him," she told me afterwards.

My father rented a private dining room in a nice restaurant in Pretoria to celebrate our engagement and where the future in-laws met for the first time. It saddened me to think how differently Hendrik's parents received me into their family: with open arms and loving me like a daughter. I knew my father would act the gracious host but I wasn't sure about my mother. I watched her closely unsure of how she would act. Oma, who sat next to me, noticed my anxiety.

She leaned over, clasped my hand, and whispered; "Relax, it's going to be okay."

The evening turned out better than I expected. My mother was cool but polite and I was relieved.

It was not only my life that changed when I went to boarding school, but Oma's too. I was in the last year of high school, and on vacation at home when my father told me that he was helping Oma sell her farm. The farm was in decline, Oma was getting old and weary and, as my father bluntly put it, "Eltjo is not farmer material; a bit of a weakling, with no clue about the business side of farming."

He was also building a little cottage for her on our farm, next to that of her eldest daughter, Rien, whose husband, Uncle Johnny, managed the dairy on our farm.

When I next saw Oma, she was spending the last years of her life happily puttering in her vegetable garden and caring for her favorite chickens that she brought with her from the farm. Uncle Eltjo meanwhile found a job as grounds keeper and gardener at an elite boy's high school in Pretoria and was happy there. Oma died in 1957—two years before our wedding. Hendrik presided over her funeral and spoke movingly of "Our Oma" at the service. Her three daughters took her ashes back to Groningen and scattered them on the land of the old family farm where she and Opa began their married life in 1912.

I will always remember with gratitude how my mother looked out for me after

Oma's death. After the funeral service she gave me the gold bracelet that Oma had worn since the day she married Opa.

"Oma wanted you to have this," she told me.

How much she maneuvered and manipulated her siblings to let me inherit the most valuable family heirlooms, among them the large linen cabinet, a wedding gift from Oma's parents when she married Opa in 1912, that she brought from Groningen in 1928, I can only guess at. ("Ida is the oldest grandchild and mother wanted her to have all her valuables.")

What I value the most is Oma's gold bracelet, a tangible reminder of her loving care and guidance through my childhood and into adulthood. She became my guardian angel. I put the bracelet on before every journey, near or far, to keep me safe till I got home again. And never did I need my guardian angel more than on the day Hendrik died in a tragic accident. When I was finally alone late that night, I searched for something to hold on to, something that would help me get through the shock and grief. I took Oma's bracelet out of my jewelry box, put it on and to this day have never taken it off.

A Day on a South African Farm

4 am. Joseph the cow herder lets out three short sharp whistles that cut through the still night air. "Hort, hort . . . hort, hort," he sings as he walks ahead of the black and white Holstein cows. Their heavy milk-rich udders sway as they follow him with plodding steps—as they do every morning—to the stable for milking. Moonlight glows faintly on the cows, outlining their shapes in the dark. It's still two hours before the moon gives way to the rising African sun.

7 am. Saara and Alena, the two black housemaids, walk into the kitchen. The smell of wood-burning smoke from their compound still clings to their clothes. They return Mamma's greeting with a timid, "Morning Miesies." Saara starts cooking porridge for the black servants, then makes a large pot of tea. Pappa will soon be coming in for breakfast.

Alena is already busy cleaning the house. I sit on the floor in my favorite corner of the kitchen, dressing my doll while my younger brother, John, pushes a toy truck, "vroom, vroom," around the table legs. No school today.

Mamma gives her orders for the day. "Saara, I want two jugs of milk from the dairy this morning, it's time to make yogurt again. And there's enough cream in the pantry to make butter later."

Saara nods. "Yes Miesies."

"Oh, and tell Buller to come to the kitchen," Mamma shouts as Saara walks out the door with two empty jugs.

We hear her outside calling, "N'Tateh!"—as she fondly calls Buller, "The Miesies wants to see you."

The old gardener comes to the back door, floppy hat in hand. My mother hands him a beaker of tea and a jam sandwich, and tells him she wants two chickens killed. We are having guests for mid-day dinner tomorrow.

10 am. Coffee time. My two uncles— Reinder, who manages the pig farm and Johnny, who manages the dairy farm—leave their dirty shoes outside the kitchen door then shuffle on their socks to their usual places at the table. Reinder—a solid, shy young man—is my mother's cousin and new to the country. He came from Groningen only a year ago to work on Pappa's farm and learn about farming in South Africa. Johnny—fat, jolly, not very clever, but with a heart of gold—is married to Mamma's older sister, Rienje.

The rest of us are already seated: Pappa at the head, Mamma to his right. John and I, at the children's end of the table, drink "pretend" coffee: warm milk laced with a few spoons of coffee and sugar. A large platter of Dutch spice bread smeared with fresh butter stands ready.

Pappa, speaking in their native Groninger dialect, asks each uncle how his day is going so far. They don't waste words.

Reinder: "One of the young sows dropped eight piglets this morning. She trampled two of them before I could get to her. I put her in the sow pen, so the rest of them are safe." His eyes brighten. "They look healthy; already fighting to get on her teats." He laughs.

Pappa nods his approval, pleased with Reinder's enthusiasm.

Johnny reports to Pappa, "I put the bull in the holding camp with four cows this morning. They—" A sudden loud squawking just outside the kitchen stops him mid-sentence.

We all look through the window. Buller has two struggling chickens in one hand, their feet tied with string. The men continue their conversation, but I'm fascinated and curious.

"Come, John," I call, "Let's go outside and watch what Buller's doing."

He ties the squawking chickens, heads down, on a low hanging branch of a tree close to the house. Wings flapping frantically they try to fly away. It's no use. A firm grip of the head, a quick thrust of a sharp knife through the beak into the brain, a last feeble flutter of wings, and the chicken hangs there, motionless. Blood drips from its beak. Buller moves on to the other chicken. We go back into the house, no longer interested in how he removes the feathers then cuts them open to remove the intestines.

4 pm. The second milking time of the day. Uncle Johnny is off for the afternoon; Joseph is in charge of the milking in the stable. Pappa sits in his office reading. Mo-ietsie, a stable boy, knocks on the office door.

"Baas!" Baas, you must come!" he calls loudly.

"What's the matter?" Pappa asks.

Mo-ietsie explains, "Joseph says one cow has a big belly, she is sick, you must come."

Pappa immediately knows what the problem is: the cow has had too much freshly cut Lucerne, her stomach is dangerously bloated, her life in danger. It's too late to call the veterinarian who lives thirty miles away. Pappa walks to the stable, trocar and cannula in hand. John and I beg to go along.

"Okay," he says, "but you know the rules."

We do: no running about or loud noises in the stable. Cows are milked in a quiet environment. A sudden loud noise can panic them into a stampede.

Just outside the stable door are two large buckets of hot water where the milkers have to wash their hands before milking the next cow. Joseph points out the bloated cow to Pappa: her back legs are loosely tied together—to prevent kicking—her head is in a halter.

Pappa moves between her and the cow next to her. He strokes her flank to keep her calm. Joseph stands at her head, rubbing it gently. Pappa feels the bloated belly, then carefully pushes the sharp trocar through the thick skin till it's in the stomach. He pulls it out and we hear a soft hiss as gas escapes through the hollow cannula. A valuable cow has been saved.

"No more Lucerne, Joseph," Pappa orders. "Take the cows to the grazing camp in front of the house when you've finished milking."

John and I get back to the house just in time to see Buller drape a dead four foot long snake over the branch where he had slaughtered the chickens this morning. He found the Egg Eater snake in the chicken coop when he gathered eggs—his last job every day before he goes home.

With a sly grin he points to the snake. "That's *my* chicken meat."

He laughs when we pull up our noses in disgust, walks to the kitchen and puts the egg basket on the counter.

Sundown. All the workers have gone home. A peaceful quiet has settled over the farm. Mamma and Pappa sit on rattan chairs in the garden, sipping sundowners: a glass of sherry for Mamma, a scotch and soda for Pappa. John and I, already in our pajamas, tumble around on the cool grass. From the camp in front of our house comes the grist-grist sound of grazing cows. Beyond the dirt road and the camp we see the lands of lush growing Lucerne that stretch down to the valley where Saara lives, up to spacious veldt and low hills that disappear in the distance. I lie on my back on the grass and look at the darkening sky. Up there, far away, the Milky Way gradually brightens as the last sunlight fades below the horizon.

"Come children," Mamma calls, "Time for supper and bed."

We run to see who gets to the door first. We're having our favorite supper: freshly picked corn cooked in milk, with lots of homemade butter. The buttermilk is used the next morning on our porridge.

Night. I wake up late in the night. The distant sound of rhythmic heartbeat de-dum-te-dum of drums—the ancient call of Africa—fills the night air. I know it well: Saara, Joseph, all in the compound, are communicating in song and ritual dance with the spirits of their ancestors.

The steady drum beat lulls me back to sleep.

And at four o'clock tomorrow morning Joseph will walk to the grazing camp and, again, let out three short sharp whistles.

NOTE:

Sow pen. An iron crate with bars in which a sow is confined for a few days to prevent trampling the newborn piglets while they suckle.

Trocar and cannula are medical instruments. The trocar with a sharply pointed end, often three-sided, that is used inside a hollow cylinder, the cannula, to introduce into body cavities.

Saara's Story

No one, not even Saara, knew the exact year of her birth. One thing is certain: it must have been at a time when the stars were aligned just right to produce a black girl-baby who, throughout her life, was for many like a gift from God.

Saara's story is embedded in my memory like an incomplete mosaic of bright bits and pieces and others faded by time. It is cemented together by her own words, my mother's and mine during the almost 45 years she was part of our family.

Saara was a Tswana, a tribe closely related to the Sothos, of Lesotho, South Africa. Tswanas spoke the same language, Sesotho, had similar tribal customs and claimed a common ancestor, *Mogale* (Adam). Their society was guided by *Kgotla*, the traditional court of laws ruled by chosen tribal elders, and by *Bademo* (pronounced Badeemo), the metaphysical powers of their ancestors. And they believed in *Modemo* (pronounced Modeemo), the Great God or the Great Spirit. Like all black babies, Saara was born on the floor of a mud hut, probably around 1920, the youngest of seven children. Her mother was helped by two older women, who cleaned her and her newborn baby up. Saara was cradled in her mother's arms to nurse and sleep till she was about twelve months old. The hut was one of several that clustered together in a compound, surrounded by a mud wall, high enough to keep cattle and goats out and toddlers and roaming dogs in. Saara's birth was celebrated in the traditional manner. Her father picked out the fattest goat in his flock, and took it to a remote place where he cut its throat with a sharp knife and let a cupful of the blood soak into the soil. This was done in gratitude to the spirits of the ancestors who lived underground for giving him a healthy baby girl. Then he skinned it and handed it over to the women in the compound to roast over a fire, and afterwards everyone feasted on goat meat and *Putu* (a thickened cornmeal porridge). The men drank homemade beer, but before the first swallow they poured a small amount on the soil in honor of the spirits of the ancestors.

The landscape of Western Transvaal where Saara grew up was similar to ours, only twenty miles away. It was vast gently undulating veldt, where in early days white settlers staked out farms by riding on a horse one hour from north to south and one hour from east to west. And if you walked far enough you would come to boulder strewn hills and see a rare leopard resting in the shadow of a crooked thorn tree, watching antelope grazing on the open grassland.

It was some distance west of those hills that Saara's father took her one day to a place called Rysmierbult (white-ant Ridge) to live with her mother's oldest sister, Sarah.

"How old were you then?" I asked her. She didn't know.

"I was this high," lowering her hand to the size of a four-year-old child.

"Did you cry when you had to stay there?"

Surprised at my question, she laughed. "No, I was a gift to my aunt, because she had no children of her own. She became my mother. I had to sleep with her in winter to keep her warm, carry water to her when she was thirsty and sweep the floor of the hut." So began Saara's working life.

In her tribal society everyone took loving care of infants and toddlers. Schooling in tribal customs, taught by women and older girls, started at an early age: how to greet and address their elders in the proper way—lower their heads and avoid eye contact, as a sign of respect; how to act when receiving a gift—cupped hands stretched out, a softly spoken "thank you," and to sing, clap hands while they danced, stomping their little feet on the hardened compound floor, in the heartbeat rhythm of drums during festive ceremonies.

Small children ate separately from adults. They ate food from the same bowl with children their own age. Older children took care of smaller ones, taught them children's games and played tricks on them. They showed them how to create clay animals and to weave branches of shrubs to make a miniature *kraal* (corral) to hold them in.

"My childhood was happy," Saara said once. No wonder: she was part of a nurturing community to which she also contributed her share as she grew older.

Soon Saara began to help herding goats, guided by older girls. Boys herded cattle. At sundown, wielding a stick twice her size, she herded them to a sturdy enclosure of tall woven twigs to keep them safe at night.

"I learned to milk the nanny goats," Saara told me one morning while we were sharing a breakfast of Putu porridge and thickened sour milk.

"What does goat milk taste like?" I asked.

"Like goat's milk," she teased. "No, we poured the milk into a pouch made of goat skin and hung it on a branch of a thorn tree to thicken, to eat with Putu."

The older girls showed her where to find *Morogo* (field spinach) and how to pick prickly pears. There were other stories: "We would smear animal fat on a stick, poke it in an anthill—that was a lot of fun—to see how many ants we could catch."

"You ate ants?" I asked.

"Of course," she replied, amused by my obvious disgust, "But we fried them first." "We ate snakes, too," she added. "When one of the boys caught a large snake, we sat around an open fire and watched it cook on the embers." I never asked her what snake meat tasted like.

And other times, when a dark cloud of locusts rained from the sky to wreak havoc on the crops of the white farmers, the women and children ran to the land with shouts of excited glee, gathered them in any container they could find, threw them into the cooking pot and had a feast. Or in early spring when fat green Mopane worms—"*Nottos*" in Sesotho—fell to the ground gorged with the blossoms of Acacia trees, everyone snacked on cooked, protein-rich, sun-dried *Nottos*. (Mopane "worms" are not worms but a kind of caterpillar.)

As she grew older Saara took on more responsibilities: one was to carry a baby strapped to her back, while its mother worked in the white farmer's kitchen a mile away, walking there several times a day for the mother to nurse it.

She learned to make brooms with shrub sticks to sweep the compound; worked the small plots of planted corn with a hoe; grinded the dried kernels with a stone to make meal; walked miles to fetch water; and gathered wood and made a fire to cook Putu in an iron pot.

Later she learned to mix equal amounts of cattle dung and wet clay to smear on the floor of their hut and the patio floor, using an old comb to make a zigzag pattern. When the floor was dry it was hard as cement.

In her early teens—about fifteen or sixteen—Saara had to leave the safety of her small community and go out into the world to earn a living. The only way was to find work with white people. I don't know when or how she finally made it to our farming community. If she told me, I have forgotten.

She must have been about nineteen when I first saw her. I was about four years old when my mother and I visited my grandmother on her farm two miles away from ours.

Saara was washing laundry in the back yard, bent over a wash board when my grandmother called her. She stood up, a tall statuesque young woman with a lovely ebony smooth face. To this day her warm smile and unselfconscious charm remains vivid in my memory as the brightest piece in the mosaic of her story. Her eyes spoke sense of humor, her voice a mellow alto.

A year later she arrived on our farm to work full time in our house. Her first baby strapped to her back by then. For me Saara brought more than just her labor, she brought her tribal culture, and language and taught me many things. I am in part the person I am today because of who she was. And she called me "Tidda," her special name for me.

One morning I found her on her knees rhythmically buffing the front doorsteps while she hummed, "Hallelujah, Hallelujah."

She greeted me in Sotho, "*Dumela Tidda, wena okai?*" (Hello, Tidda, how are you?)

I replied, "*Dumela Saar, na ke teng, wena okai?*" (Hello, Saar, I am fine, how are you?)

I was curious how she got her baby. She sat back on her haunches and looked to the sky.

"God sent a biiiig white airplane right through the clouds and down to the veldt where that old mud hut stands, you see it?" She pointed to the ruins of a hut across the valley. "Then an angel got off the plane with my baby and left it inside the hut."

"What did the angel look like," I asked, thoroughly intrigued by her tale.

"He was dressed in shiny white clothes and had wings like a bird."

I still wasn't satisfied. "How did you know your baby was there?"

"Oh," she said without blinking an eye, "God sent me a dream long before to tell me."

I liked her story much better than my mother's who had to go to a nearby town and wait two weeks to get my baby brother.

Saara and I frequently had breakfast together, sitting on the grass in the warm sun, sharing a bowl of dry cooked *Putu* pap (corn meal porridge) and *dik-melk* (thickened sour milk).

But it was not just sharing food that was important to me. I created a game to make it real, and Saara played the major role in it. I transformed from white child to young black woman with a baby, my doll, tied to my back. We spoke her language, Sesotho, not mine. And I had to ask for work at the white farmer's house in order to eat.

So when Saara saw me waiting at the garden gate early in the morning, she greeted me with: "*Dumela Oussi,*" (Hallo, sister), and asked how I was. I returned her greeting in the ways of her tribe, looking down to avoid her eyes as a sign of respect. Calling me "sister" made me her equal, an honor not often bestowed on a white person, let alone a child. But for as long as the game lasted, I was her younger sister. (I was unaware then that I was also picking up on the importance of ritual that brings people together.)

We had to go to the back door. I waited outside while Saara told my mother that a stranger was looking for work. My mother too, played her part. She kept a straight face when I told her that I was good at dusting but not much else. Only then was I allowed inside to help with cleaning under Saara's strict supervision. Dusting for two hours was boring, especially since I was not allowed to play in the process. The only thing that kept me at it was the reward of, at last, having breakfast with Saara.

Sharing the same bowl of porridge was a ritual too, the oldest taking the first bite then down the line to the youngest. Alena, the other woman who worked in the house, was the oldest. She would take a small amount of porridge in her right hand, pressed it into a lump then dipped it in the thickened sour milk and put it in her mouth. Saara was next and then it was my turn. It was a simple meal but I loved it.

Sometimes, in the early summer, Saara would bring a small package wrapped in newspaper for our breakfast. I sensed what was coming by the sly amused way she looked at me. She offered me what was in the package: cooked, sun dried "*Nottos.*" It was a seasonal protein-rich delicacy that black people loved. As always, I took one look and instantly, conveniently, became a white child again so that I didn't have to eat such disgusting stuff. If I were a black woman, I would politely take one and eat it with relish, but at that point I would get up and leave, followed by Saara and Alena's loud laughter. Breakfast was done.

The father of her son was a proud Zulu, Joseph Makatane. They were not yet officially married, but following tradition Saara changed from wearing short dresses to ankle length dresses. This was a sign to other men that she was no longer available.

Choosing a man from another tribe was the first indication that Saara was her

Travelling Beyond Borders

own person, not tied to tribal tradition where marriage to a distant relative was the norm. She had found a man she could respect, always expressing her love for him with spontaneous joy. He was clever, could read and write, worked in an office in the big city, Johannesburg, and earned more money than an ordinary farmhand. He had found a gem: a loving woman who bore him a son.

Another indication that Saara was her own person was in her choice of her son's name. Instead of a "white man's name," as it was called, she named him Stokane, a black man's name. Her next son was named Skweree and her daughter Manamee. "But," as she told my mother, "he can't claim his son until he brings *Lobola* to my family." And in the years following his son's birth, that's exactly what Joseph did.

Every second weekend Joseph would travel by train from Johannesburg, fifty miles away from our farm, to visit Saara who lived in a hut in the compound where all the farm laborers who worked on our farm lived.

When I was about sixteen years old, Saara told me that Joseph (who had visited her that weekend) told everyone in the compound that there was a young man named Nelson Mandela who was agitating for the end of Apartheid. Neither Saara nor I knew exactly what that meant but I told her that Mandela would probably not succeed, because Apartheid was now a law. We never talked about it again.

(Mandela was arrested in 1964 and sentenced to 27 years of imprisonment on Robben Island, an island separated from the Cape mainland by some seven miles of shark infested sea. He was finally released in 1990. That was the beginning of the end of Apartheid. In 1994 Mandela was elected president of South Africa.)

When Stokane turned twelve years old, Joseph took him to a remote area of a neighboring farm to be initiated into manhood. Women knew not what went on there, but Joseph later told Saara that somewhere behind the low hills in the distance their sons were undergoing three weeks of harsh initiation.

On a day when only a shimmer of the rising sun was visible on the horizon, three women approached the gate of the fenced-in land. Warm colorful blankets protected their bodies from the winter cold. Two, Miriam and Anna were barefoot; Saara wore old, discarded shoes of her missus.

Two days ago the women had placed bowls of Putu, tightly covered with a cloth, beside the fence. They knew their sons were undergoing harsh initiation: how their young sons were circumcised with a rough blade, and told not to cry in the process; slept naked in the open veldt, covered only by animal skins; hunted for meat with a club—else there was only dry Putu; taught tribal laws by their elders, the responsibilities of manhood, and to respect and heed the guiding spirits of their ancestors. Close to the fence the women saw two empty bowls; the third still had Putu in it.

An untouched bowl of Putu left by the fence was an age old tribal tradition, sending a silent message to a mother. Anna's son was dead. Infection, fever, and severe cold had done its job. The women each took her bowl and walked back to the compound.

Later, at sundown, a tribal elder went to Anna's hut; he told her, "Your son's spirit is now with those of his ancestors. You must not weep for him, Mma." With her head bowed low, Anna nodded.

When I was thirteen my parents sent me to a girl's only boarding school in Pretoria where I stayed until graduation. I only went home for holidays and an occasional weekend in between. My letters home were filled with homesickness and stories about my classmates.

By age fifteen I went through the usual mood swings of most teenagers, obnoxiously loud one day and weepy sentimental the next. It didn't change when I went home. One morning when I was in a particularly obnoxious angry mood, I went to my bedroom and saw that my bed wasn't made. Ignoring the fact that I had to make my own bed at the dorm every day, I marched to the kitchen and yelled at Saara that she had better make my bed right now or else. Saara said nothing, went to my room and made my bed. For the rest of the day she was quiet, made no jokes, and ignored me.

When I realized what I had done, I was overcome with shame and remorse. For the first time in our relationship I had treated Saara like a servant. I felt sick and sensed that I had rashly destroyed something very precious.

Saara's silence continued the next day. I didn't know what to do. Late in the afternoon I couldn't stand it any longer, I went to the dining room, took half a slab of chocolate, put it on the kitchen counter and put my arm around her.

She didn't thank me, only looked at me with a warm smile and said, "Oh, Tidda." My awkward plea for forgiveness was accepted, and I was, thankfully, back in her good graces. After that, I always made my own bed whenever I was at home.

I had learned a very painful but important lesson that day: even a servant, particularly a black one, had a measure of dignity and was entitled to respect from a white person.

Her three children were in their teens when Joseph came home to visit Saara one weekend and complained that he was not feeling well. Early the next morning someone found his body in the outhouse, apparently from a sudden heart attack.

Sometime later, Saara told me with a sad smile, "He was such a proud man. It was so humiliating to die with his pants down."

I told her that he was probably not even aware of this when he died.

My father had set aside a small plot of land, a peaceful spot under tall shady trees not far from the compound, where farmhands could bury their dead. That's where they buried Joseph, his body wrapped in a clean blanket, no coffin. There were no markers of who was buried where. The body no longer counted. It was the spirit that joined the realm of his ancestors that mattered.

Saara quietly mourned Joseph's death. When we met again several years later, she told me, "I have so many good memories of Joseph. I was blessed to have had such a good and loving husband."

I was nineteen years old when I met the man who would eventually become my husband. My parents did not approve of my choice.

My mother: "He's so short, not even handsome."

My father: "If you marry this Bible toting student of Theology you will live in abject poverty for the rest of your life."

Then I introduced him to Saara. It was probably the first time in her life that a white man took her hand and greeted her in Zulu.

She responded with warmth, *"Dumela Moruti,"* (Hallo, Pastor), covering his hand with her other hand in tribal greeting, with eyes lowered. Then she looked into his eyes and saw the man I fell in love with: warm, caring, and solid.

Our wedding was a grand social event. All the important people filled the church and the reception tent under the trees in our garden. The gifts were expensive and splendid.

But it was Saara's gift that moved us the most. As we walked down the garden path towards the reception tent, Saara suddenly appeared from behind the house, still wearing her kitchen apron. She greeted us with jubilant song and the Sotho tribal dance of wedding celebration till she was before us. Then she danced backwards, tears running down her cheeks, sweeping the path with a cloth, a symbolic gesture of clearing away any obstacles that could possibly hinder a happy life together.

Her celebration dance over, Saara disappeared to the back of the house. I ran after her and caught up with her in the kitchen. I hugged and kissed her and thanked her.

She hugged me back and whispered, "Be happy, Tidda."

In 1969 my mother called and told me that my father was selling the farm because his health was deteriorating. They planned to move to a quiet neighborhood in Johannesburg where they were building a comfortable house for themselves. Behind the two-car garage they also built a small apartment for Saara. With Joseph no longer living, she was happy to go with them.

Travelling Beyond Borders

In 1978 my mother called and told me that my father was diagnosed with inoperable stomach cancer and did not have much longer to live. Two days later I arrived at Johannesburg airport. My mother and brother were there to pick me up, and we immediately drove to the hospital where I managed to speak to the doctor in charge. He told me they could try chemotherapy. I knew enough about chemotherapy to know that it would not cure my father, just prolong the agony. I told my mother and brother that we should take my father home to be cared for by his immediate family for as long as he lived.

The house doctor came by to check on my father. When I told him that I was a former nurse he brought some syringes and morphine and told me I could give my father a shot of morphine in the morning and another at night. This eased the pain and allowed him to sleep better, even during the day.

My father was happy to be home, but he wanted no visitors. Only Saara was allowed, who came in every morning to quietly clean and dust the bedroom. He always greeted her with a smile saying, "Good morning, Mrs. Makatane, how are you?"

She replied with a smile saying, "Good morning, Baas."

My mother and I took turns caring for my father, every four hours, night, and day. It gave us time to rest and eat some food.

Saara was a devout Christian woman, a Baptist. Her faith was interspersed with tribal beliefs. In the white man's religion, if you were good you would go to Heaven, if you were bad, you went to Hell. In the tribal beliefs if you were good the spirits of your ancestors would give you healthy children, your crops would flourish, and your cattle increase. If you were bad your children would be sickly or die, your crops would fail, and your cattle stolen.

There were other ways in which Saara's faith in her ancestors were revealed. It was when I came to help my mother take care of my father. Saara proudly showed me the little apartment that my parents had built for her. It consisted of a living room furnished with a table and several chairs. Along one side of the wall there was a small kitchenette with hotplate, tiny sink and storage cupboard. In one corner stood a television, which allowed Saara to invite four or five of the neighboring servants to come watch programs in the evening. They had to leave before 10pm because there was a curfew: all blacks had to be off the streets by then. Police were driving around to arrest any trespassers and take them to jail.

There was a separate toilet and shower room. The small bedroom was furnished with a chest of drawers and an iron bed. Each leg of the bed stood in an empty vegetable can half filled with water. I asked Saara why she had done this.

Her reply: "This prevents the evil spirits from getting onto my bed."

I did not laugh. As someone once told me, for a non-believer the idea that Jesus Christ was raised from the dead and ascended to heaven standing on a cloud sounds just as ridiculous as putting water in an empty can to prevent evil spirits from getting on her bed.

It was in the middle of the third week of caring for my father that there was a change. It was midnight when it was my turn to sit with him. He suddenly woke up and tried to sit up. I asked what the matter was.

"I need to go to the toilet."

I told him he was too weak to get up and I would give him the urinal to use. Obviously confused, he tried getting out of bed again.

When I gently pushed him back, he angrily said, "Ida, don't be silly."

He fell back and I noticed that he was breathing with difficulty almost like gurgling, but did not speak again.

The next morning I called the doctor and told him what had happened. A little while later he walked into the bedroom and examined my father. "Your father had a stroke last night. It won't be long now." He gave my father a double dose of morphine and left. I told my mother and brother that the end was near.

They waited in the living room while I sat with my father. An hour or so later my father's breathing became slower. I called my mother and brother to come

Travelling Beyond Borders

quickly. They stood at the foot end of the bed watching him. Suddenly he raised his hand as if to wave goodbye then stopped breathing.

I was still sitting on the chair by my father's bed, holding his hand and staring at his still face. I could hear my mother crying in the living room. Soon after, Saara walked into the bedroom. She stood at the foot end of the bed and looking at my father said "Oh-Oh."

She uncovered his feet, bent down and kissed them, saying softly, "*Koebaai my baas.*" (Goodbye, my master.) That simple gesture touched me. I began to cry. Three weeks of pent up emotions and little sleep had taken their toll on me.

I felt her hand on my shoulder, "Come, Tidda, we must lay him out."

We removed the pillows together and Saara did the rest. She folded his arms over his chest and closed his eyes.

When she said, "Now we put the sheet over his face," I hesitated, still not sure my father was dead.

"He is gone, Tidda," she said quietly.

I called the doctor and told him my father had died. He came soon after to verify my father's death, and called for a hearse to move my father's body to a funeral home. Three days later, with family and friends attending the solemn service, he was cremated. Saara could not attend because she was black, and not allowed in a whites-only chapel.

A year after my father's death my mother sold their house and moved into a small house in a retirement community. This meant that Saara also had to retire. Apartheid law allowed her the choice of either going to live in her "homeland," where she had never been and knew no one, or she could move to a treeless, middle of nowhere compound consisting of some hundred houses, a small grocery store and small church, five miles away from where she had lived and worked. She chose the latter because her children were already living there.

The small house that my mother was able to buy for her consisted of two rooms: no bathroom, an outhouse in the back. My brother rented a truck to move the furniture in her apartment to her new home. (Not sure if the tin cans went with the bed.)

In the few feet that separated her house from the dusty street, Saara planted flowers. She watered them from a faucet in the road that provided the only running water for six families.

There she spent the last years of her life, taking care of her grandchildren, and walking to the dingy little church to attend Sunday services until she could no longer walk.

Saara died in 1989. I don't know how she died or where she is buried. I do know that her spirit has joined the realm of her ancestors and will remain there forevermore.

NOTE:

"*Lobola*" is translated as "bride price," a misconception perpetrated by Europeans as "buying a wife (woman)." Lobola was actually a transfer of a certain amount of cattle to the family of the bride after the families of bride and groom had negotiated the marriage contract.

Lobola was not a dowry, because the wife had no control over it. She could leave her husband for reasons of abuse, neglect or was unhappy with the marriage. The cattle stayed with her family, and in turn were used to pay Lobola when a son wanted to marry.

Paying Lobola allowed the husband to claim his children. He was also responsible for the well-being of his parents-in-law and extended family. (Derived from: *The Bantu-speaking Tribes of South Africa.* Edited by I. Schapera. 1953)

Little Buck

When my father bought a farm in West Transvaal, South Africa, in 1930, there was already an Indian shop on it. The "Coolie place," people called it. Mia's one room shop stood at the bottom end of our farm, on a dirt road that connected two small towns: one fifteen miles away to the east, the other thirty miles to the west. Besides a bakery—run by a jolly Dutchman—this was the only shop for miles around. Whenever my mother gave me a few pennies I would walk or skip rope the mile from our house to the shop to buy a handful of sweets.

Everyone, black and white went through the one door and shared space at the counter where Mrs. Mia, dressed in a colorful sari, and Mr. Mia, always polite, served their customers. The aroma of spices mingled with the odor of unwashed bodies and the smell of rolls of new cloth neatly stacked on the shelves. Large burlap bags of cornmeal leaned against the wall behind the counter; bins of loose tea stood on the shelf, next to bottled sweets; cans of paraffin for the Primus stove stood in a far corner. It was a cozy place with a fascinating other-worldly magic.

Then, as if from one day to the next, our sleepy farming community changed. A half mile up the road from Mia's shop, a brick building went up. On the covered porch a sign read Buck's General Store. Right next to it, Buck's Butchery with its own entrance. Mrs. Buck would manage the store; Mr. Buck the butchery.

The white community heaved a sigh of relief. "At last; a white man's shop. Now we don't have to go to the Coolie anymore."

For the Mia shop it was the beginning of the end: a loss of customers and, when Apartheid became law in 1948, they were no longer allowed to live on a white man's land, and had to move away. But here my father intervened.

He was a liberal thinking man, and always voted against Apartheid. He negotiated with the local authorities that if Mr. Mia paid rent, he could stay on the farm. They agreed. So, from then on Mr. Mia came to our house once a month to pay the rent. My father let him in the house through the front door and into the living room where my mother served tea and cake.

For the blacks there was a change too. The new store had two doors: one for "Whites Only" and at the far left of the porch, a door for "Blacks."

"Only two at a time allowed inside, and STAY on that side," Mrs. Buck said loudly. The rest had to wait on the porch. "They stink up the place!" she exclaimed with a sniff. People agreed.

The Bucks had three children. The youngest was called Little Buck—Bucky for short—his father, Big Buck. His mother doted on him. They looked alike: small frame and chiseled faces with large dark brown eyes: Mrs. Buck's had a sharp unfriendly look when she talked to blacks. Bucky's eyes radiated kindness and good humor, like his father.

What stood out was their darker than usual skin tint. Folks whispered: "Maybe she has black blood in her veins." or "How can a white man marry a Coloured woman?" But that was just gossip; at least Mrs. Buck wasn't as dark as the "Coolies," and everyone still went to Buck's General Store.

Bucky and I were the same age, and sat together in second grade in the two room school not far from where we lived. Like all the children we walked there, and after school played games in the dirt road on the way home.

In class Bucky was a listless pupil and didn't pay much attention to the lessons. The teacher let him be, knowing how Bucky would turn out: with so little interest in learning he would end up as a bus driver or a train conductor, clipping tickets, or work in his father's store.

Bucky came alive in the store, helping out and playing the big man whenever I was there. Often, when his mother made the blacks wait while she was making small talk with white customers, Bucky would go quietly to help them, handing the money to his mother afterwards. They liked him and playfully called him *Klein Baas*, Little Boss. For many he was like a ray of sunshine in an otherwise gloomy atmosphere where Mrs. Buck's uncouth manner and sharp tongue obliterated any sense of cozyness or magic, like Mia's shop.

Bucky failed third grade and had to do it over. By then we went to a bigger school, five miles away by bus. I lost track of him, and only saw him when my mother and I went to buy groceries.

We grew up. By age eleven I had started to develop. They weren't much bigger than a pigeon's eggs but when I stood up straight, they showed through my dress. I felt self-conscious and shy and, despite my mother's "Walk up straight, Ida," I slouched.

One day I was standing at the counter in the store watching Bucky putting groceries away, when I suddenly heard Mrs. Buck's sharp voice say to my mother, "So, Sien, I see the hornets have been busy in your house," and with a loud laugh pointed to my chest where two little buds bulged under my dress.

I felt a hot wave of shame come over me and slouched forward. Every one, I knew, was looking in my direction, amused by my embarrasment.

My mother said quietly, "Why don't you go sit in the car and wait for me, I am almost ready."

Looking down so that no one could see my tears, I walked out.

I hated Mrs. Buck, and thought of drastic ways to get back at her, somehow. Spread rumors: she was "Coloured"! She should be forced to live with the blacks she hated so much! On and on. In childish frustration I just wished that something really bad would happen to her. And I would never to go the store again, ever!

A month later Little Buck was dead. A freak hunting accident. A few men, among them his uncle, went to the far distant veldt one night to hunt wild buck. Bucky sat in the truck and, feeling very important, loaded a gun for his uncle. Forgetting to put the safety catch on he handed it to him through the window, the barrel facing him. The gun went off and Bucky was hit in the chest. He died almost instantly.

Everyone in the white community, including his classmates, attended his funeral. At the grave site I saw Mrs. Buck, a pitiful figure in black, and Bucky's father holding her close, overwhelmed with grief. By then I had forgotten any thoughts of revenge on Mrs. Buck. There was only sympathy and sadness.

After Bucky's coffin was lowered into the ground, the pastor said a prayer, then made a motion for people to make way. There, to everyone's surprise, stood a large group of black men and women. They had quietly assembled during the service. The pastor motioned them to come closer. Then they sang: a soaring black hymn in chorus that seemed to envelop us all in shared grief. When they stopped there was a moment of complete silence; everyone was moved to tears. Someone shuffled, the ranks of white mourners closed again and the spell was broken.

Life went back to normal. That sublime moment of shared grief by a group of black and white people over the death of a little boy, soon faded into vague memory. Or quickly forgotten. I never saw Mrs. Buck again, but sometimes I wonder if she looked on blacks more kindly after her Little Buck's funeral.

For the Mia family life improved considerably. Most of the black people went back to Mia's shop again. The Bucks soon realized that they had lost many customers and eventually had to close shop and move away.

Medicine Woman

None of the stories my mother read to me in my early childhood scared me. Not even the one of the wicked witch who lived in a sinister forest waiting for little children to get lost there so she could eat them for supper. That was because the witch was safely tucked away on the pages of *Grimm's Fairy Tales*.

I had my own real witch to cope with. Folks said she lived in the woods adjacent to our farm, but I was never sure about that. Her sudden appearances out of nowhere, and disappearances—sometimes for several months—added to the mystery of who she was and where she came from. Nevertheless, every time I saw her, I was paralyzed by fear. The blacks called her a *Sangoma*—Medicine Woman—but we called her Mad Meana, the Witch Woman.

It was a warm summer afternoon when I first met her. I was five years old, and my black nanny Lisa and I were sitting in the shade of tall Eucalyptus trees beside the dirt road that passed by our farm. We were drawing pictures with sticks in the cool sand and speaking Sesotho, the language Lisa taught me from the day she arrived when I was a toddler.

Suddenly, the figure of an old black woman appeared in the distance. She was talking and singing incoherently to herself while she veered from one side of the road to the other as if she was drunk. I had never seen her before and pointed to her.

Lisa said, "She's a Witch Woman. Nobody knows her name. When she comes close, you have to get up to show respect, lower your eyes and say, '*Dumela Ngono*' (Good day, Grandmother), not '*Dumela Oussi*' (Good day, Sister) like you greet me. If you don't greet her properly, she will grab you and carry you away."

As Meana came closer we could hear the rhythmic shish-shish sound of dried seedpods around her ankles as she walked. She ignored my greeting, only asked

Lisa who I was. While Lisa explained in a quiet respectful voice, and pointed to our house behind the trees, I took a closer look at her. She had a wrinkled face with eyes that stared vacantly into space as if she were lost in a world of her own. Her filthy dress was in tatters. Around her neck she wore an assortment of wires, animal bones tied to strings, beads, and feathers. More feathers were stuck helter-skelter in her kinky hair. I was fascinated: how could such an odd looking, filthy person command so much respect?

It was my first lesson on how you can't always judge a person on appearance only, but what others make of them.

For the next few years this mysterious figure was part of my childhood. And I wasn't the only one. All the kids, black and white alike, were afraid of her. There was never any indication that she was in cahoots with the devil or in any way evil, but stories about her were fanned by black folk lore and our childish imagination. It was said that if she found a kid walking about alone, she would catch it and put it in the large sack that she always carried with her. What she did with such kids we could not imagine.

Sometimes when my younger brother and I were playing with our black playmates on the dirt road, Mad Meana would suddenly appear out of the woods, climb over the barbed wire fence and walk towards the black compound down the road.

In childish bravado, since there were quite a few of us, we would tauntingly yell "Hey, Mad Meana, where are you going," or "Are you mad, Mad Meana?"

She would walk on, muttering to herself or sing in her usual way, veering from side to side on the road. Then suddenly she would lunge in our direction with an incoherent cry and we would scatter with yells of excited fear. There was nowhere to run except down the road or towards our house but we never ran that far, instead, laughing at each other's fear, we stopped at a safe distance and kept on taunting her.

At age six I had to go to school. The two-room school was about a mile away down the road to where another dirt road crossed it, and about half a mile beyond where the blacks had their compound. It was the road Mad Meana usually walked and I was the only kid to walk that road, twice a day.

But I didn't have to worry too much about Mad Meana for a while. She had disappeared again and with the newness of school, I forgot all about her. Until suddenly one day the rumor went around that Mad Meana was back!

From then on, I kept a sharp look out for her whenever I walked back home from school. And sure enough, out of the blue one afternoon, I saw her figure in the far distance just as I got on the road to our house. Luckily the shack of Paul the black shoemaker was close by, so I ran into it for safety.

Paul, a friendly old man greeted me with a cheerful "hello," and asked how I was.

"Oh, I just wanted to say hello," I said, and asked him about the shoes he was repairing.

Of course, I didn't want him to know that I was hiding from the Witch Woman walking towards his shack. So we talked on until the woman came close and I saw to my relief that it wasn't Mad Meana, but Maria, Paul's daughter carrying her baby on her back. I said a hurried goodbye and went on my way home, cheerfully swinging my book bag.

It was quiet and peaceful while I walked—only an occasional moo of a cow in the distance disturbed the stillness—something about living on a farm that I still miss. Lost in thought, I suddenly heard a rustling sound in the woods close to me. Then the familiar rambling talk of Mad Meana and her sudden cackling laughter that made me jump with fear. I was petrified. There was no one in sight. No one who would hear my cries for help if Meana caught me and put me in the sack she was carrying over her shoulder. Not even the occasional car that sometimes drove by leaving a trail of dust was in sight.

By then Meana had climbed the fence—with more agility than I thought possible for such an old woman—and walking towards me. The only way out was to get over the barbed wire fence into my father's farmland—opposite from the woods—and escape that way. I threw my book bag over, hitched up my dress and put my leg over the middle wire of the three wire fence. Just as I bent down to crawl through, my panty caught on the top wire. I was stuck and Meana was coming closer and closer! In desperation I twisted my body and pulled away from the wire to free myself. The barb ripped my panty and I felt the burn of a scratch on my bum. But I was safely on the other side and started to run. I heard Meana laugh in what sounded like a real witch's cackle. When I looked around, she was already walking down the road without so much as a glance in my direction.

My mother wasn't happy about my ripped panty and didn't believe my story of how scared I was that Mad Meana was going to carry me away in her dirty old sack, and that I would never be able to get back home.

"You're just imagining things again," she said.

Meana was real. She was in fact a harmless, homeless, and confused old woman who found shelter in the woods and went around begging for food. My childish imagination and stories about her had created a scary witch who added drama and excitement to my childhood.

But then, children never tell their parents everything. My mother had never heard of Mad Meana before.

The End of an Affair

I don't remember exactly what made me fall for Frankie when we first met. He was tall, good looking, with straight black hair and large brown eyes. Aah yes! Those mesmerizing eyes that spelled mischief and sly humor when he looked at me. Or was it his infectious laughter? Whatever it was, I was smitten.

And then, he was so clever. He knew everything about farming, he said. So much that even I, a farmer's daughter, was impressed. I watched in awe as he demonstrated—with a hint of self-assured swagger—how he wielded a whip on a team of oxen, or the firm grip he had on the steering wheel of a monster tractor while he plowed the fallow land in a straight line.

If only his father would let him. He was seven years old; I was nearly six, and not yet in school. We lived on neighboring farms, separated by a dirt road at the bottom end of our farm.

It was on the same road a half mile farther up that led to the school where Frankie was already in second grade when I started in the first. Before that, whenever we were together, I was not so much a playmate as a captivated audience of one, while he bragged about how, "I know all about school, and you don't," adding ominously, "The teacher is going to hit you with a ruler everyday if you don't do your sums right." He never got hit; he was too smart.

My mother told me a better story. "Wouldn't you like to read Cinderella and Snow White all by yourself?"

I loved all the fairy tales my mother read to me: Prince Charming coming to the rescue, or the Ugly Toad transforming into a Handsome Prince, with princesses who wore lovely dresses.

I was a little unsure about the sums and other things I had to learn in school, or sitting at a desk and not allowed to play till the afternoon. But a new dress, shiny black shoes, and that I would see Frankie every day made up for being confined in a classroom.

My mother took me to school on the first day. It was a small two-room building with a corrugated iron roof, shaded by a towering tree, the yard fenced in to keep wandering cows from the neighboring farm out, and the children in. Close to the fence, in a corner, stood a shabbily constructed, smelly outhouse, its wooden door kept closed by a hook in the doorframe. We all knew about outhouses; almost everyone used "the little house" at home.

There were two teachers and some 25 pupils, from first to eighth grade. Master Kerling, grey-haired and dapper, was the principal. Strutting about, he would proudly survey his small domain of school yard and outhouse as if he were the executive of a large company. He was obviously fond of children, strict but kind, and passionately dedicated to their education.

Every morning Master Kerling stood in the doorway that connected the two classrooms and read a few verses from the Bible. Then we all prayed "Our Father Who art in Heaven . . ." and so our day started.

I sat in the front row with six other first graders in Miss Brett's class, who taught the first four grades. She smelled nice, was always calm, and didn't use a ruler to hit the children, like Frankie said. She had a more formidable weapon: Master Kerling and his switch, seldom used, but visible in the corner as a constant reminder to "Behave!" So when she said in her usual calm but firm voice, "Frankie, if you don't stop fooling around right now, I'm going to send you to Master Kerling," Frankie instantly sat still at his desk.

I liked school, but saw little of Frankie. He sat in the back of the class, and when we were on the playground, he had a bigger audience to impress. That didn't bother me much; everything about school was new and interesting. Miss Brett told us stories from the Bible, we learned to add, "Two and two is four," to write the ABC neatly, and sing nursery rhymes, "Mary had a little lamb, little lamb . . ."

Travelling Beyond Borders

In the last hour of school every day, each grade had a turn to stand in front of the class and recite a poem or sing a song. Friday was story time when Miss Brett read a story to the whole class.

It was on the day when we first graders had our turn and were singing, "Baa, Baa, Black Sheep, have you any wool . . ." that disaster struck. Miss Brett suddenly stopped us in mid-song, looked at me in astonishment and said in a loud voice, "Ida! What are you DOING?"

I looked down; my face flushed bright red with shame. There, running down my legs, spilling over my new shoes, a puddle of pee was growing ever bigger as my uncontrollable bladder emptied itself onto the floor. The whole class erupted in loud gleeful laughter, and I started to cry.

"Hush now," Miss Brett said to the class, took me by the hand and led me out the door. Outside she asked, "What happened, I thought you went to the little house before?"

Between sobs I explained that I couldn't get the hook off to open the door and there was nowhere else to go, not behind a bush or anything. She walked me to the outhouse and unhooked the door, but saw that for a little girl—frantically trying to hold it in—the hook was high and difficult to undo. She put her arm around me and told me to stay out in the warm sun till it was time to go home.

When the children came outside some giggled in passing, others teased me, "The baby peed in her pants, ha-ha." Frankie's voice was the loudest.

From a safe distance he danced around taunting me, over and over, in a sing-song, "Ha, ha, Ida peed in her pa-hants, pa-hants." His once bewitching laughter, now humiliating me.

In angry frustration I picked up a clump of dirt and threw it at him, only to see it break into pieces at his dancing feet.

And with that, my imaginary affair came to an end. Frankie, the Handsome Prince of my little girl dreams instantly transformed into an Ugly Toad.

Getting Religion

The year I started second grade a new family named De Beer moved into an old, abandoned house across the dirt road from our farm. "You will have someone to play with now," my father said. That was good news. Most of my playmates lived a mile or more away. Now I could just cross the dirt road that ran along the length of our farm, climb through the wire fence, walk a short distance through the forest and there, in a clearing, stood the house of my future playmates.

My mother refused to climb the fence. She took the car, drove to the other side of the forest, and made her courtesy call. A half hour later she left with a these-are-not-my kind-of-people look on her face.

A clue was the sparsely furnished living room: no welcoming comfortable chairs with soft cushions; instead we sat on hard chairs around a large table covered with oil cloth. A long wooden bench stood against one wall. It was the glassed in haloed face of Jesus above it that put my mother on guard. Seriously religious Afrikaners lived here.

Mr. De Beer, a low level official of the Blyvooruitzicht (Happy Prospect) Gold Mine Company—five miles away—was a friendly slightly built man with nothing to say and completely overshadowed by his wife's enormous size and no-nonsense manner. Their two daughters, Rena, my age, and Deborah, a year younger, matched their mother's rotundity and the meekness of their father.

Then there was Miss De Beer: slight, like her brother, flat chested, dress down to her ankles, lace-up shoes, mouse colored hair in a tight bun, and not a speck of humor on her pious face.

Unlike my mother I came away with the happy thought that I would now have companions to walk to school with. Better yet, Miss De Beer would walk with us. They didn't know of my paralyzing fear of Mad Meana who roamed the forest looking for lonely children to carry away in a sack. Now she wouldn't dare come close.

So every morning, with a starched hanky tucked in her belt, and carrying a little suitcase, brimful with sandwiches for the girls in each hand, Miss De Beer led the way to school. In the afternoon, there she stood again waiting at the gate in the shade of a tall tree to walk us back, carrying the now empty suitcases.

As the weeks went by though, I became more disillusioned with my new playmates. No playing on Sundays. Not allowed to take off their shoes to play in silky mud puddles after a rare thunderstorm, or climb a haystack and slide into a pool of loose hay, never play hide-and seek in the cornfields, or swim in the muddy water of the earth dam on our farm. Large platters of food made up for the loss of joyous childhood play.

It was Miss De Beer who fascinated me. She seemed to live in another world, as if her special connection to God made her so staidly serious, so good, so disciplined that even her walking was measured, each step exactly the same as the next. How did it feel, I wondered to be so religiously devout? In my childish mind I didn't know how to get there. Mimicking her walk didn't help, and neither did a starched hanky.

One day I asked Rena why her aunt always walked with them to school and back. She shrugged her shoulders slightly and said, "She's afraid that kaffirs will do bad things to us."

I looked at Rena's porky body and wondered what the blacks could do to them. I did not understand their fear. I had no fear of blacks. except Mad Meana. and felt comfortable around them. Ever since I was six years old, I roamed around the farm or the dirt road on the way to school on my own. I spoke their language, Sesotho, always greeting them with *"Dumela, wena okai?"* (Hallo, how are you?), and was greeted in turn with a friendly smile.

As the weeks went by, I realized that Miss De Beer never took any notice of me, or hardly greeted me. I asked Rena why her aunt didn't like me.

"Because you don't go to church," she replied.

True: there was no religion in our house, not even a Bible. All I knew about religion were Bible stories told by the teacher in school and saying the Our Father. Our family's sins were multiple: we were Dutch, church-avoiding "invaders" from Holland; my parents regularly went dancing in the Blyvooruitzicht community center; my father smoked cigars; and in the peaceful hour before sunset he and my mother would sit on rattan chairs in the garden, my father with whiskey and soda in hand, my mother sipping sherry, while my brother and I tumbled around on the sweet smelling grass in our pajamas, till tired out, we would lie on our backs and watch the stars making their appearance in the darkening sky. In the peaceful quiet we could hear the grist-grist sound of cows grazing in the camp across the driveway of our house. None of this seemed like sin to me.

But I did commit one sin: beating a girl I didn't like on her shins with a stick. She cried and I was happy. My mother spanked me and locked me in the bathroom.

I asked my parents if I could go to church with the De Beers on Sunday.

My mother said, "No! I hate those sanctimonious types."

My father, ironic humor intact whenever my mother sputtered angrily about her dislike of Afrikaners, said, "Oh why not? Let her go."

When Rena heard this, she asked if I wanted to come to Sunday school with them before church. Miss De Beer was the teacher, and I had to learn two Bible verses for class. My parents bought me a Bible.

Our two room school converted to a church on Sundays. Old men with long beards and coats, women with unadorned black hats, sat on the school benches, and listened to a lay preacher's fervent sermon and long winded prayers. I didn't understand half of it. There was singing too: a lead singer began with a long drawn out lament to God, followed with more wailing by the congregation. Not a note of joy.

Travelling Beyond Borders

How different was the church of Saara, our black housemaid, and her people. They had no church building to go to. The blue domed sky was their church.

On Saturday nights they would sing and dance to the rhythmic heart-beat de-dum-te-dum of African drums to communicate with the spirits of their ancestors, a traditional form of religious ritual that went back many centuries. And in the early morning hours on baptism Sunday we could hear from afar the same de-dum-te-dum of African drums coming closer and louder up the road towards our house. Then singing, dancing as they sang, Saara and her people, praising Modemo (God) in jubilant chorus, their steps keeping to the beat of the drums all the way to the dam at the top end of our farm. I followed them, running through the land to the dam where I sat screened by the low branches of a weeping willow tree to watch the baptism.

I didn't like the somber service of the Afrikaner church. I felt out of place, not like the De Beer girls whose tiny voices wailed along with the adults and bowed their heads low during prayer. But I still wanted to go to Sunday school. My parents said it was okay.

For a month or so I dutifully learned the two assigned Bible verses; my mother coaxed me when I got stuck. Miss De Beer seemed pleased, even smiled at me sometimes. She told stories about the good deeds of Jesus and how He was crucified on the cross for our sins.

One day she told us how our various sins added to His "continual suffering." Forgetting to learn our Bible verses, she said, made Jesus very sad. I felt guilty. And, "Sewing on Sunday is the same as thrusting a needle in the eyes of Jesus. Blinded, and the blood running down His cheeks! Isn't that a terrible thing to do?" she asked, sobbing at the image.

Horrified, I ran home to tell my parents. They were in the living room; my father reading the Sunday paper—another sin—my mother working on her embroidery. I told her to stop immediately; she was a sinner, piercing the eyes of Jesus with the sharp needle! And all that blood! My parents looked at me in stunned surprise.

"Utter nonsense," my mother finally said angrily, and continued embroidering.

My father, not amused this time, said, "I don't think you should go to Sunday school anymore."

I was relieved: no more boring Bible verses to learn, or hear Miss De Beer's depressing stories. I didn't want to be religious anymore. It was all too difficult and confusing.

Relief was followed by dilemma: I had to choose between walking to school with her, always aware that I was a doomed sinner, or walk alone in constant fear that Mad Meana would suddenly appear on the road and carry me away.

But then Providence stepped in and I was saved. Another family had moved into our area, across the road from the De Beers. We were now four who could walk to school together and, happily, Miss De Beer stayed home. Mad Meana still roamed the forest but that didn't bother me: I could run faster than the De Beer girls.

And I had a new friend, Marthie Perrit, who could climb a haystack and slide down into a pool of loose hay, even on a Sunday.

Section III:
From High School to Nursing School

Destiny

The Girl with a Pearl Earring

Remembering a Humble Man

A Most Unusual Pet

How I became a Nurse in South Africa

China Blue Cups

Destiny

Through the years I often marveled at the intricacies of human relationships: how one person's choice at a crossroads in life, or a sudden seemingly unrelated death, can affect the destiny of another. So it was for me.

On a quiet Saturday afternoon a man got up from the dinner table, walked to the living room, and fell down dead in the doorway. The man was the father of my best friend, Marthie Perrit. We were twelve years old on that tragic day in 1948.

Her father's sudden death brought about a drastic change in Marthie and her family's life. It was only many years later when I realized that his death also changed the course of my life in an unexpected way.

Marthie and her family moved into our farming community when I was in the third grade. There were not many children nearby for me to play with, so we soon became best friends.

Their house was one of several in a compound that belonged to the Blyvooruitzicht Gold Mine Company five miles away, when gold was discovered around 1938, and where the town of Blyvooruitzicht was gradually developing. Mr. Perrit headed a small team of mechanics who fixed the trucks and cars of officials of the company. The other residents were a team of five bookkeepers who lived and worked in offices on the premises.

The Perrit house was so small that Marthie had to share a bedroom with her frail grandmother. We lived in a big house with a large garden. I had my own bedroom with toys, and a bookcase filled with children's books in English, Dutch, and Afrikaans. There were no books in the Perrit house, only a large Bible from which Marthie's grandmother read a chapter every evening after supper, and her father said a long prayer after. We had no Bible and never prayed.

My parents were Dutch immigrants from the Province of Groningen who spoke in the Groninger dialect, but Afrikaans to my brother and me. Despite their English sounding family name, the Perrits were fervent Afrikaners. Like many other Afrikaners who remembered the humiliating defeat of the Anglo-Boer war, they had not much love for anything English.

We, on the other hand, were pro-English. My father subscribed to English newspapers, my mother read *The Woman's Weekly* that came all the way from England and I was a devoted admirer of the Royal Family—even arranging objects on my desk to look like that of Princess Elizabeth in a photo.

Despite our cultural differences—Marthie could not follow me into my English play world—we created our own magic world of "house-house," and tea parties with our dolls. By the time we were nearly twelve years old, our games became more serious. Our favorite game was "teacher and pupil," reversing roles each time, and the back yard was our classroom.

To look like and be an effective teacher, we believed, required boobs and long hair. Marthie had an advantage here: she had inherited her father's naturally curly black hair—worn to the shoulders, and her mother's Barbie doll figure. Her boobs were already the size of pears. I was flat, and had straight blond hair cut to just below the ears. I begged to let my hair grow long, but my mother always said NO. No amount of sulking changed her mind.

"It would not suit you," she said, and that was that.

How was I going to get long hair? Marthie couldn't help me there. One day I suddenly spotted the wooden clothes pins on the wash line. Marthie helped me clip about ten of them to my hair all around my head, and voila, I had long hair almost to my shoulders.

But I still needed boobs.

"Why don't you use oranges?" Marthie suggested when I told her of my problem.

That was a brilliant idea; I stole two oranges from the dining room and put them inside my dress. (How they stayed up there is still a mystery to me.) And so we played for hours. At the end of our game we sat on the grass and sucked the juice from the oranges till they were dry.

Our childhood games soon came to an end, however. High school loomed ahead. There were no high schools in our area, which meant going to a boarding school in a town, 25 miles away. Marthie saw it as an adventure—she was a straight A student—I was more insecure about leaving the cocoon of safety I grew up in. I got mostly B's, rarely crossing the B border to an A. Marthie soon persuaded me that it would all turn out well, we would still be together, and maybe even share a room. That made me happy.

My happiness did not last long.

"We want you to go to the English high school," my father told me one day.

This was a blow. Every subject from biology to history I had learned in Afrikaans would now be in English.

"I don't want to go to an English school!" I cried.

My father patiently explained: with an English education I would one day be able to leave South Africa and find a future in England. or Australia—anywhere where English was spoken. I was not interested in leaving the country, my home and family, I said.

I was thoroughly unhappy. Marthie consoled me as best she could. "At least we will be in the same town and be together during vacation."

Till that quiet Saturday afternoon when her father died and our lives changed. Several weeks after her father's funeral, Marthie and her family moved back to Pretoria, where they had come from, fifty miles away.

A month after they settled in Pretoria, Marthie wrote that she had been accepted in the Afrikaans Girls High School, the Afrikaans Hoer Meisies Skool—A.H.M.S for short, for the following school year. It was a boarding school too, she added. That was enough for me. I rushed to the living room to tell my parents that I wanted to go to a boarding school in Pretoria.

"It's an Afrikaans school," my father said.

"I know," I cried, "but Marthie is there, and I want to be with Marthie."

"Let me think about it," my father replied.

The agonizing wait lasted two days. On the evening of the second day, my parents came home from a visit with Master Kerling, who had known me since the first grade when he was the principal of the two room school in our community.

Master Kerling was on my side. He persuaded my parents that A.H.M.S. was an elite school, where I would be in good company with the daughters of cabinet ministers, and other important people in the South African Government. That clinched it for my father. I could go to Pretoria! I wrote Marthie the good news. Of course, I would be staying in the dorm, and she was a day student, but we would still see each other.

Her reply was a lukewarm, "That's nice," which, in my excitement, I completely missed until I got to Pretoria.

Marthie had changed in the six months since we last saw each other. She returned my enthusiastic greeting and hug with a calm, "How are you?" and then introduced me to her new best friend. I was devastated.

Luckily that did not last long. The new school, settling into dormitory life, and meeting new roommates quickly did away with my sadness. I made friends with other boarders, among them another Marthie—a farmer's daughter just like me—and ended up with five Best Friends. "The Gang of Six," we called ourselves.

We even had a motto: "Life is not what you want, but what you have. So take it, put a feather in your hat and be HAPPY!" We stayed together till matriculation.

We all passed with grades good enough to apply to the University of Pretoria. But I didn't want to go to University, I told my parents. I wanted to go to nursing school, a dream I had since I was five years old.

"No," my father said, "Nursing is what lower class girls do. You will be better off studying to become a teacher."

I dutifully applied to the University, and got accepted. Life confined to a dorm, however, did not appeal to me. My friend Marthie, whose much older brother,

Hendrik, was studying for his Master's degree at the University, got her a room in the boarding house where he lived. Maybe Marthie could ask him to get me a room too? My parents said okay.

Marthie called me at home. "My brother doesn't want to get a room for you. He says he doesn't want to be responsible for another female juvenile."

I was desperate and boldly called him one afternoon, almost pleading with him to get me a room.

"Okay," was all he said.

A few days later I got the good news: there was a room available, but I had to bring my own furniture and linens. My parents were great; they did everything to make me comfortable in my first independent living quarters, including an electric water kettle to make instant coffee and a tin full of homemade cookies from my mother.

That's how I met my future husband.

In time Hendrik became my best friend. He saw me through the worst when I failed every subject in the first year including my favorite subject, English. I had brought shame and embarrassment on my family, and when my father said, "all that tuition money down the drain," my guilt developed into severe depression. I did not want to be a teacher. But when he later said, "I'll give you another chance," I dutifully went back to University.

One day, soon after classes started, I broke down and told Hendrik I was very unhappy. I had no interest in becoming a teacher; I was just not cut out for that kind of career.

"Here's what you can do," he suggested, "Write a letter to your parents and tell them exactly how you feel and that you really want to go to nursing school." He read the letter, "Excellent! Now let's go mail it together."

Holding my hand all the way to the post office, ceremoniously helped me drop the letter in the mailbox.

Then he said, "Come, we have to celebrate this. I'm going to take you to a small café and treat you to some coffee and éclairs."

I don't remember if I fell in love with him on that day, but eventually I did. It took him much longer to wake up and decide I was the one for him.

My mother called a few days later to say that she and my father were very moved by my beautiful letter and that I could go to nursing school. I dropped out of University the next month, applied to the College for Nurses, got accepted, and went back to dorm living. In this case my father did not have to pay any tuition fees, or even give me pocket money because nursing schools were government supported, and student nurses were paid a small monthly salary, just enough, for example, to buy a pair of shoes, and toiletries when needed.

About four years later I passed the final exams at Nursing College with flying colors. My parents were proud of me.

My father got his wish: I did leave South Africa, but not the way he had planned: settled in England, and married to an Englishman. Instead, I ended up marrying Hendrik, an Afrikaner with a PhD, who landed a job in the USA as Professor of New Testament Theology at Emory.

And reflecting over my early life I sometimes wonder; if Marthie's father hadn't died on that day, where would I be today?

NOTE:

It took Hendrik some time to decide I was the one for him. He was still trying to overcome his grief when the young woman he was hoping to marry broke up with him for another man. Her name was Betsy. I was a first year student at the high school for girls and she was in her senior year and a straight A student, winning many awards.

And here is another twist in the story. I was in my senior year in nursing school, and had to work for three months in the operating room to prepare for final exams. One day toward the end of my time there, a woman was rushed into the operation room in critical condition. Among other things she needed a blood transfusion. The right kind was not immediately available, and when they finally found the right blood, it was too late. She had died on the operating table. That woman was Betsy's mother!

The Girl with a Pearl Earring

The loan of Dutch painter Johannes Vermeer's famous *Girl with a Pearl Earring* (dated 1665) to the High Museum in Atlanta from the Mauritshuis Museum in The Hague several years ago, prompted me to send my three daughters a story of how I first met their father, Hendrik Boers.

I was a senior in Afrikaans Hoer Meisies Skool in Pretoria in 1953, and shared a room with three classmates in the dormitory. One of them was Marthie Boers, Hendrik's younger sister. She was tall, blonde, and buxom with the dream of one day becoming a famous concert pianist. The boys in the neighboring Boys High school were crazy about her.

Hendrik, in his 4th year as a student of Theology at the University of Pretoria, lived in a Singles Only boarding house not far away.

Marthie and Hendrik's parents were farmers who owned a farm near the small rural town of Ermelo, a two hour trip by train, south of Pretoria. Though not exactly poor, they had a limited budget. They paid the rent for Hendrik's room, and furnished it with the minimum of furniture: a desk, a chair, a bed—which functioned as sofa during the day—and a few bookcases. His monthly pocket money was enough to pay for one meal a day at the dining room of another boarding house a few blocks away that catered to students and government employees. During the four years that he lived in the boarding house, Hendrik gradually turned the bleak room to a more homely one. The only way he could do this was to save as much as possible from his pocket money by periodically skipping meals, and living on bread and coffee. His first purchases were two large replicas of Dutch paintings, both framed with an elegant unadorned wooden frame: the *Laughing Cavalier* of Frans Hals and Vermeer's *Girl with a Pearl Earring*.

In those four years Hendrik also kept an older brother's eye on his "baby" sister, Marthie. When the boarder girls were allowed to go home for a weekend—"leave after school on Friday, be back by 4pm on Sunday,"—he would travel with her on the train to visit their parents on the farm.

On the last of these midterm weekends, we noticed that Marthie had not returned by four pm on Sunday. On Monday, still no Marthie. We asked, "where is Marthie?" No one knew.

On Tuesday morning at school assembly the principal, Miss Steyn, told us that Marthie, her parents, and older brother, Hendrik, were in a car accident over the weekend. It happened at night on a country road when the car hit a big truck that was illegally parked on the side of the road, and rolled over into a ditch. The car was totaled but, except for some bruises, no one was seriously injured. Marthie had fared the worst; all her front teeth were knocked out by the impact. She would be back in school as soon as the dentist in Ermelo had fitted her with a set of false teeth.

"I hope you will all treat Marthie with kindness and understanding when she returns next week," Miss Steyn continued. "You can imagine that any damage to a girl's face at this age must be emotionally traumatic."

A week later Marthie was back. Other than a few fading blue marks on her face, she looked the same. But she had changed in another way. The effervescent, cheerful Marthie had become a somber, self-conscious unsmiling girl. Her close friends didn't know what to do; none of us had gone through a similar experience. Someone else came to the rescue.

On Friday afternoon, when I was alone in the dorm room there was a knock on the door. It was the House Mother looking for Marthie. I explained that she was at her piano lesson.

"There's someone with a package in the visitor lounge who wants to see her. Maybe you could go down and get it."

A young man with very dark hair and warm brown eyes holding a big package wrapped in brown paper, got up from a chair when I entered the lounge.

"Good afternoon," he said in a rather formal tone. "I'm Hendrik Boers, Marthie's brother. Could you give her this please?" He handed me the package.

"Of course," I said.

He thanked me and left. It was only afterwards that I remembered I had not introduced myself to him. He had no idea who I was.

When Marthie came back from her lesson she looked with surprise at the package on her bed. I told her that it came from her brother who asked me to give it to her. She carefully removed the paper, and there it was: the framed *Girl with a Pearl Earring* that he bought for himself a few years ago and which she always admired. She looked at the painting as if seeing it for the first time, then rested her head on the frame and started to cry.

"He's such a good and loving brother," she said.

I realized later that it was probably the first time since the accident that Marthie was able to have a good long cry. It relieved her from all the pent up emotions she had struggled with for almost two weeks. From then on, she gradually became more like her old self.

She carried the painting with her for the rest of her life, through many years of an unhappy marriage to an abusive husband, a wealthy farmer who owned a big house and a Cessna airplane. He was in his mid-forties when he died after crashing his Porsche into a tree speeding at 120 miles per hour. She was left penniless except for a small sum of money to pay the rent for a small house and keep his five underage daughters clothed and fed till they reached matriculation.

To supplement her income, she gave piano lessons to several students. The rest of his money went to a married woman he had an affair with.

Till the last day of her life "Girl with a Pearl Earring" hung on the wall in Marthie's bedroom opposite her bed. It was the last thing she saw when she died of inoperable cancer a few months after her 60th birthday.

Remembering a Humble Man

(Or, the Journey of a Brave Man)

It was a sunny day in the suburb of Sunnyside, Pretoria. Rays of sunlight filtered through the colored windows of East Church as a tall young man with solemn face climbed the few steps onto the pulpit. He stood there quietly for a moment looking at the congregation as if to say, here I am, your new pastor.

East Church stood solid and grand in the middle where two streets met in the shape of a boomerang. It was surrounded on two sides by the grounds of my school, the Afrikaans Hoer Meisies Skool—A.H.M.S for short—and across the University of Pretoria campus. Wealthy people lived close by.

It was the year 1949. I sat on the gallery, wearing a white dress and white Panama hat, just like my fellow boarders of A.H.M.S. school. I was fourteen years old. Below sat the congregation: a mix of cabinet ministers of the South African government, officials, residents of the surrounding neighborhood, and professors from the University. Theology students, their blazers of navy, wine and gold, conspicuous among the somberly dressed congregation, filled the rows of benches in the back. Among them sat a 23-year-old first year student listening intently to the pastor while he preached and prayed with quiet passion.

The church elders had chosen well. Beyers Naude was a rising star in the Dutch Reformed Church and his future promised a major role in its hierarchy. He was also appointed chaplain for the University of Pretoria.

"I liked what he said then and the way he talked about faith," my future husband, Hendrik—that first year student in the back row—told me when we met four years later when I was a first year student at the U. of Pretoria. "I sensed an immediate chemistry when we shared liberal ideas about religion at a private student/chaplain session."

I agreed, "He inspired me so much that I decided to attend his catechism classes and become a member of the Church."

At that time it was indeed a big step for a fourteen-year-old whose family never went to church or prayed at home.

What I didn't tell Hendrik until many years into our marriage was that the chemistry I felt for Beyers Naude was different from his. My "conversion" had nothing to do with religion or joining the church, and everything to do with my developing hormones. I had a severe crush on the man. Of course at that age my naïve girlish dreams ignored reality: he was married and the father of two children.

No one, not even his wife, who listened to Beyers Naude preach that Sunday morning knew that he had come to a religious crossroads in his life. He was beginning to doubt the Dutch Reformed Church's justification that Apartheid was part of God's plan.

He grew up in a conservative Christian house, where his father, Jozua Naude, taciturn and absolutist ruled family life. Like most Afrikaners, Jozua developed a fierce hatred for anything British after they lost the Boer war against the ruling British. He was one of the cofounders of the Afrikaner Broederbond (Brotherhood)—or AB —in 1915, who firmly believed that the Afrikaners were planted in South Africa by God. "We are God's chosen people," sounded from pulpits throughout the land. It was their God given task to further Afrikaner nationalism, to maintain Afrikaner culture, develop an Afrikaner economy, and to eventually gain control of the South African government which was at that time a member of the British Commonwealth.

Two years after the end of WWII, AB had become so politically strong that it gained control of the South African Bureau of Racial Affairs (SABRA), and where the concept of total segregation—Apartheid—was developed. By then Beyers Naude was also a member of the AB.

It was when he took a six months trip to Europe and the USA as an emissary for the Dutch Reformed Church that his eyes were opened. He was stunned to discover that he knew nothing about the other side of Apartheid. People asked him about Albert Luthuli, president of the African National Congress—considered a subversive movement by the government, and later the winner of the Nobel Peace prize in 1961. Naude had never heard of him. Nor did he know anything about Alan Paton's *Cry the Beloved Country,* a novel that created a sensation overseas for its stark portrayal of the effects of Apartheid on the black population. There were other questions that Naude had no answers for.

Back home he started to study the biblical, theological, and historical justification for Apartheid that his church had promoted. He found none.

"I was devastated with the discovery, and what it meant for the future of the church and our country," he told us in 1963 when he visited us during another tour through the US sponsored by the American Friends Service. We arrived in Atlanta the previous year when Hendrik was appointed Prof. of New Testament at Emory. Sitting in our small living room, his wife Ilse Werder—the daughter of a German missionary—next to him on the sofa, he described what life was like for them. "You wake up with it and you go to bed with it, shunned by everyone, even close family, living in isolation most of the time."

It was fourteen years before that Hendrik and I first saw him on the pulpit of East Church. There had been no further contact between us until their visit in Atlanta. It was only then that he heard that we were former congregants of his church. The young man who inspired so many people with his sermons had aged prematurely. At 48 years old, his face was wan and showed signs of a man burdened by a nearly hopeless battle to single-handedly change the course of the Dutch Reformed Church. If the church moved to eliminate Apartheid, he reasoned—for blacks the rights to share the *responsibilities, rewards, and privileges of citizens*—the Afrikaner people would follow. But no one listened . . . yet. Instead he was ostracized by most of his fellow pastors—a few who thought likewise, remained silent—shunned by the Afrikaners, and condemned as a traitor by the politicians. Among them Hendrik Verwoerd, his former teacher of Social Studies at the University of Stellenbosch, Cape Province, who became prime minister in 1958 and known as the "Architect of Apartheid."

When they said goodbye, Naude's last words to us were, "I might never see you again. The authorities are threatening to revoke my passport. So, if you come to South Africa, come for a visit." We never had the opportunity. When we got there in 1975, he was already under house arrest in a Johannesburg suburb, and only allowed one visitor at a time.

Undaunted by the ostracism of his fellow citizens, Naude, his faith in God strong, continued his mission: he founded the Christian Institute in 1963 as an ecumenical movement hoping white churches in South Africa would join in eliminating Apartheid. Except for the Catholic Church, very few did. He walked out of his own church when it condemned the Christian Institute as a heretical movement, and gave up his membership of the Afrikaner Broederbond.

He visited blacks who lived in slums of fenced-in concentration camps, bordering the city premises. How did they, ordinary blacks, cope with Apartheid? At first the blacks mistrusted him; a white Afrikaner appearing in their midst and asking questions? But, ever courteous, mild mannered and pastoral, he finally won them over. Black pastors invited him to come and preach in their churches. Nothing Beyers Naude did was ever political but others did not see it that way.

In the early seventies the government banned the Christian Institute, declaring it a subversive movement, like the ANC, that would lead to terrorist uprising among the blacks. Naude, with his passport revoked, was put under house arrest with police surveillance 24/7. Nothing he said was to be recorded or printed.

His restricted movements did not prevent him from doing what he set out to do, however small. He quietly fixed old cars and small trucks in his backyard and passed them on to blacks to ease their transportation.

Visitors, one at a time, were allowed to visit him. One of them, Desmond Tutu, a rising star in his black community, and future recipient of the Nobel Peace prize in 1984, wrote after a visit, "Beyers Naude is the most resplendent sign of hope in South Africa today."

Shortly before his house arrest Naude spoke to an audience at the University of Cape Town:

If you truly love your country, then decide now—once and for all—what kind of country you wish to give yourself to and then commit yourself to see to it that you have a share in the way such a country is being created and built—even if it eventually has to be built from the ashes of a society which has destroyed itself through its own blindness, its avarice, and its fear. A new South Africa is being born—a South Africa in which I wish to live . . . a South Africa in which I wish to give myself to all the people of our land.

In 1984 Naude was released from house arrest, and on May 10th, 1994, he sat on the podium to see Nelson Mandela inaugurated as President of the "New South Africa." Not far from him sat Tandi Gcabashe, the daughter of Albert Luthuli, the man whose name Naude did not know when he started on his venture.

On September 7, 2004, the long journey for Beyers Naude came to an end. He was given a state funeral.

NOTE:
Beyers Naude was among the many white South Africans to be incarcerated for his anti-Apartheid activities. His ancestors, the Naude's, were French Huguenots who settled in the Cape in the 17th century. There are many buildings, streets and other areas in South Africa named after Beyers Naude. For instance, the Beyers Naude square in Johannesburg.

A Most Unusual Pet

His name was Jackie. "He's a real character and very amusing," my mother said over the phone, telling me how happy she was that she had taken Jackie in to live with us on our farm in South Africa. He had adjusted quite nicely into the family circle since his arrival three months before.

So imagine my surprise and disappointment when I got home from boarding school and he ignored me when I said a cheery hallo, as if I wasn't there.

"Don't worry," my mother whispered, "He'll come around soon; he's just shy of strangers."

The next day I found him on the patio, alone, and tried again: "Hallo Jackie, how are you?"

Still no response. I stood around for a while trying to get his attention but when he kept on ignoring me, I turned and walked away. Suddenly I heard him say, "Birds can't talk."

I laughed and said, "You can too, you silly parrot."

I was fifteen years old and in boarding school in Pretoria when I met Jackie for the first time. By the time I went back to school, he had stolen my heart, and like everyone else's, had it firmly tucked under his wings. He was part of our family for the next thirty years.

Jackie was an African Grey parrot with an attitude. My mother rescued him from a bar owner in a neighboring town. All Jackie had learned while cooped up in his cage in the barroom was a rhyme of dirty words, the mildest of which was "You damn bastard."

My mother would have none of that. Every time he started, she would say sternly, "No Jackie!" and gradually the dirty words faded from his memory, except, "You damn bastard," which he used at times with great comic effect.

Travelling Beyond Borders

From his cage on the patio—where he spent most of the summer—he had a grand view of the garden and the cultivated land that disappeared from view in a valley a mile away.

Every day at sunset he was brought into the house where his cage was put in a corner of the living room. From there he could see into the dining room, part of the front hallway, and hear what was going on in the kitchen.

He learned most sounds by association: timing the squeak of the refrigerator door when the maid prepared our lunch. Sometimes he would call out to the kitchen door, "Jackie wants nuts!" He also picked up the on the Groninger dialect that my parents spoke.

For instance when my father walked in the front door at ten o'clock in the morning he would call out in my mother's voice, "*Wolstoe koffie hebbn?*" (Do you want coffee?) followed with "*Joa,*" (Yes) in my father's sonorous voice.

When my mother was nearby, he would begin singing in her voice, "Let me call you sweetheart, I'm in love—" then abruptly stop.

She would sing along with him, "I'm in love with you."

He would start again, stop, mutter something, then laugh at himself, as if to say, "I don't remember the rest."

Jackie showed his flair as trapeze artist when he and my mother danced together. She would say, "Let's dance Jackie," and lift up her arms.

Jackie spread his wings wide, and followed her movements, first kicking his left leg out, then the right followed by a flawless pirouette on his perch, and start over again. After several turns my mother would bow her head and say, "Thank you." which Jackie acknowledged with a regal bow of his head.

When we had visitors he sat quietly on his perch, sometimes muttering softly to himself while the conversation went on. His usual shyness of strangers made him mute, and no amount of coaxing could get a sound out of him. All he did was ruffle his wing feathers neatly together, and settle himself more firmly on his perch. Until one day when the new pastor of the Dutch Reformed Church came for his obligatory visit. My mother fled to the kitchen, leaving my father to deal with the pastor.

Afterwards my father—who never attended church—entertained us with his story of how he patiently listened to the pastor's whining voice: "Oh, Mister John, you must come to church; just think of the afterlife; there's a hell waiting for every lamb that strays from the flock," and so on.

Until my father had had enough of it and interrupted him; "Okay Reverend, I'll come to church if you provide me with a rocking chair and serve coffee halfway through the sermon; is that a deal, or would you accept a check?"

The pastor accepted the check, stood up to leave when suddenly my father's voice came from the direction of the cage.

"Buzz off . . . You damn bastard!"

After a stunned, embarrassed silence my father started laughing, and the pastor, his sense of humor intact, laughed too.

One day I had the idea to teach Jackie my special bird whistle: Twee-Heet, Twee-Heet. From then on it was the way we communicated. I discovered later that he only whistled this way when I came home after several months away.

It was on one of my visits home that I noticed that Jackie pulled out one of his tail feathers and used the sharp end to scratch the top of his head. I asked my mother about it and she said she had noticed it too and asked the veterinarian about it. The veterinarian told her it was sign of frustration for being cooped up in his cage all day, and she should let him out of his cage several times a day when he was in the house.

Jackie was very happy it seemed as he hopped from chair to dining room table and hiding under the coffee table which was covered with cloth that reached to the floor in the living room, as if he knew that after a while my mother would call him to get back in his cage. He always gave himself away when he called out in my mother's voice, "Come Jackie, back into your cage!"

Years went by; I got married, and in the same year moved to Germany where my husband studied for his PhD, and I had a baby. When my baby was nine months old my father became critically ill. I went home to be with my parents and introduce them to their first granddaughter. My father recovered and we took him home.

I found Jackie in his usual place on the patio. I whistled a few times. No response. I wasn't surprised: he had forgotten me in the almost two years since we last communicated. But there was something new to attract Jackie's curiosity and attention: my daughter who spent a lot of time on the patio in a play pen. She in turn was fascinated by this strange, feathered thing that talked to her.

One day while I was in the kitchen, I suddenly heard the familiar whistle from the patio. I rushed out and found Jackie arranging his feathers, but couldn't get another whistle out of him. All he did was demonstrate a new sound he had picked up: my baby daughter's crying.

At some point during the years that Jackie was with us, my father sold the farm and he and my mother moved to a house in a Johannesburg suburb, taking Jackie with them and where he learned to imitate city sounds among them the yapping bark of the neighbor's little dog.

About five years later my father died so my mother sold the house and moved to an apartment in Pretoria where no pets were allowed. He stayed with my brother's family for a few years, till my mother found a kind veterinarian who specialized in small animals including parrots who took loving care of Jackie until he died several years later, leaving our family with fond memories of a remarkable pet.

How I Became a Nurse in South Africa

Before I could read I already knew that I was going to be a nurse when I grew up. There's no doubt in my mind that I got the gene from my grandmother. She was the one who helped put a cloth diaper of my baby brother on my head so that I would look like the veiled nurses at the local community hospital, some four miles from our farm. I wore it when I operated on my dolls (Meaning, smearing Vaseline on their tummies) or bandaged their limbs.

My mother didn't take me seriously. She just laughed; reminding me of the times I had fainted at the hospital because "it smells funny," or vomited when the nurse approached me with a syringe to give me shots against mumps, measles, and whooping cough. It was true: I was a source of embarrassment to my mother when that happened.

But I did finally make it to nursing school: an untested, naïve nineteen-year-old when I entered the Andrew McColm Training Hospital in a wealthy suburb of Pretoria in 1955. Nursing colleges in South Africa were government sponsored and separate from Universities. Tuition was free and by working in the hospital we earned a small salary, beginning with about seven pounds a month in the first year and increasing to about twelve pounds in our senior year. In those days it was enough to buy a pair of shoes, a dress and toiletries.

Nursing school wasn't exactly like the *Nurse Cherry Ames* books by American author Helen Wells that I absorbed during my teenage years. Instead, we wore starched white uniforms and caps, and underwent a British military style kind of training, reminiscent of nurses training during WWII.

"Roll UP your sleeves when you attend to patients; roll DOWN your sleeves when a doctor addresses you; stand at attention against the wall when Matron—head nurse of the hospital—approaches."

Travelling Beyond Borders

And to distinguish us from other students in training, first year students wore a plain white belt, in the second year a white belt with a thin blue stripe, and in the third a blue belt. For three and a half years I would be exposed to daily human drama, and trained to cope with it, physically and emotionally.

In the first months of college we learned "Theory of Nursing," and took turns washing a dummy patient in bed. Points off if you spilled water or soapsuds on the sheets. We took photos of classmates smooching with the floppy skeleton in Anatomy class. We practiced giving shots on oranges; only to discover later that the human butt doesn't have the same consistency. Little details like keeping "input and output"—"drink and pee"—charts; and, before the time of disposables, how to sterilize catheters, syringes, and a host of other hospital instruments including setting up sterile trays for dressing wounds; rolling bandages correctly; down to examining feces; and the proper way to clean a bedpan. And at exam time trying to remember which medicines to use for a mind-boggling array of illnesses—Quinidine, "for auricular fibrillation not accompanied by heart failure," or Phentolamine for "pheochromocytoma," (try to pronounce that!), a rare adrenal gland tumor—drummed into our ears, and hearing over and over, "Remember, one mistake and you're OUT!"

After each semester our teachers let us loose in the hospital wards, and the operating room to practice what we had learned. That's where we were confronted with the reality of what nursing is all about. Most of us pulled through, others couldn't cope and left. Only a few stark memories of those years in nursing school, and the patients, doctors and fellow nurses who affected me, remain. Time obliterated the rest.

My love affair with Freddy became the talk of the hospital staff. It was love at first sight when he cheerfully told me, "I have spinal meningitis." Big words for a four-year-old to say. He had the face of a cherub, big blue eyes, and thick blond hair. His mother lived a hundred miles away and rarely came for a visit. I became his devoted slave: waiting on him hand and foot, taking his temperature, washing him, feeding him, and giving him his medicine.

When he needed me, he would call, "Nurse Ida, come here!"

No matter where I was, his small voice reverberated loudly through the hallways till I showed up. Other nurses who responded to his calls were met with, "I want Nurse Ida," and that was that.

Things came to a head one morning when his calls began to sound frantic, and the nurse in charge told me to drop what I was doing and go to him. "He won't to tell us what the problem is."

I rushed to his room and found him jumping up and down, holding on to the rails of his cot.

"What's the matter?" I asked anxiously, expecting something serious.

"I need to pee," he wailed.

The next day his doctor told us Freddy was ready to go home. I never saw him again.

A newborn baby with multiple birth defects died in my arms. I had never seen anyone die before.

In today's world a baby born with a cleft palate, hydrocephalus (water on the brain), no thumbs or big toes and no rectum would be fed intravenously and undergo multiple operations to create a semblance of a normal human being. Back then the pediatrician prescribed only that we feed him small doses of milk from a pipette, and let nature take its course. That was my task.

It was while I held him, squeezing a few drops of milk at a time on his tongue when he suddenly made a small choking sound and stopped breathing. I didn't realize immediately what had happened. Then came feelings of shock and guilt; I had killed the baby. A little later the pediatrician came into the glassed-in cubicle and found me sobbing over the crib. He put his arms around me and spoke in a soothing voice. It was bound to happen and definitely not my fault. After I

Travelling Beyond Borders

calmed down, we looked at the malformed body and the gaping hole where a small mouth was supposed to be.

"It's almost a blessing that this little creature died," he said. "The most difficult job for a pediatrician is calling the parents and telling them the bad news. There's the tragedy."

It was in the operating room that my future career as a nurse almost came to an end. I was a junior nurse and functioning as a low level gofer, learning the ropes of operating procedures. An elderly woman lay on her side on the operating table waiting for the surgeon to perform a lumbar puncture. My job was to hold her down to prevent her from moving while the surgeon injected a local anesthesia. When he carefully pushed the long needle into her spine to extract the spinal fluid she started moaning in pain. The anesthesia had either not taken yet or was not enough. I felt very sorry for her, but couldn't do anything except hold her down. But then long forgotten childhood phobias: the heady smell of ether, syringes with long needles, flooded over me.

I fainted. On top of the patient.

I came out of it when I heard the doctor's angry voice in my ear. "Nurse, what the hell are you doing?"

I started crying, thoroughly embarrassed and apologized over and over. Someone took me by the arm and led me out of the operating room. I sat on a chair in the hallway thinking about my future and I knew: it's all over. After a while the surgeon came out of the operating room, smiling this time.

I said, "I guess I'm not cut out to be a nurse after all."

He bent over me, and patting me on the shoulder, said, "Oh no, far from it, it's the kind of person who feels acutely and can sympathize with the pain of others who makes the best nurse. You're okay." With a final reassuring pat, he walked away to get ready for the next operation. My future was back on track.

Another memorable incident happened in the operating room when I was functioning as a gofer. A young male patient had to undergo an appendectomy.

My task was to pick up all the used swabs that the surgeon threw on the floor. I stood at the head end of the operating table to watch the proceedings. The patient was already under anesthesia. The head nurse stood opposite the surgeon. Her task was to hand him all the surgical instruments he needed. The patient's body was already covered with sterile sheets except the genital area. When she touched his penis to move it out of the way it suddenly grew bigger. The more she slapped at it the bigger it grew until it stood straight up like a flagpole.

I had never seen anything like this before.

Suddenly the surgeon looked at me with an amused smile and asked, "First time nurse?"

I felt myself blushing and looked down, totally embarrassed. Everyone laughed.

Then there was the patient who wanted to die. Back then there was no such thing as "a right to die" policy. "We live in a Christian country," the reasoning went, and "only God decided when and how you died."

I was a "middler," in my second year as student nurse when the issue came up. My duties started at seven in the morning and ended at seven in the evening, with only a few hours' break in between. I was assigned to a room with four female patients in the woman's ward.

My tasks included washing them—with the help of a junior nurse—change the bed sheets every day, turn them over periodically to rub their backs with cologne to prevent bedsores, spoon feed those who were not able to feed themselves, and take their blood pressure, among others. Around each bed was a curtain that could be drawn to give patients more privacy.

One day when I went on break there were only three patients in the room. When I returned several hours later a fourth patient, Mrs. Botha, had just been admitted. She was a small, elderly, severely emaciated woman, lying inert on the bed with her eyes closed, and did not respond to my greeting.

I was checking her chart when Dr. Miller, her doctor, walked in. He spoke softly while he told me her story. She was a simple country woman, the widow of a poor farmer, and judging from her small, calloused hands, used to hard work. Her children, alarmed by her obvious illness and refusal to eat, brought her to Pretoria to see him. His diagnoses indicated that she was in the final stages of inoperable breast cancer that had probably spread further into her body.

"I want to show you something," Dr. Miller said. He uncovered the woman's chest. "This is what severe breast cancer looks like." The left breast was not round and soft like a normal breast; instead it was almost square in shape. "Now touch it," he said.

I was a bit apprehensive at first, but I realized that this was what nursing was all about. The breast was rock hard, so was the swollen lymph node under her left arm: an indication that the cancer had spread, perhaps even into her brain.

Mrs. Botha remained unresponsive, and kept her eyes closed while the doctor and I examined her.

He took me aside and said, "Her children mentioned that Mrs. Botha didn't want to live any longer. All we can do now is to make her as comfortable as possible, give her regular shots for pain and feed her." He would leave instructions at the desk.

Mrs. Botha turned out to be the strangest and most difficult patient I had to deal with thus far. My troubles started on the first day when I went to feed her at five that afternoon.

"Mrs. Botha," I said softly, "it's time for your dinner."

There was no sign that she heard me. I stroked her cheek and called her name again. She suddenly opened her eyes and I looked into a pair of faded blue eyes.

"I don't want to eat," she whispered.

"You have to eat something," I said. "I brought you some mashed potatoes with gravy." Trying to coax her, I said, "You don't have to chew, just swallow."

"No!" she whispered vehemently, "I want to die." And with that she closed her eyes and resolutely pressed her lips together. Starving herself was the only way this poor woman knew how to end her suffering.

Totally frustrated, I went to the head-nurse in charge of the ward. "I can't get Mrs. Botha to open her mouth to eat."

"You have to feed her," the head-nurse replied. "Those are Doctor's orders."

"But I don't know how," I said.

"Then just pinch her nose till she can't breathe and has to open her mouth," was the cool reply. "Come, I'll show you how to do it."

I remember the following few days as the most uncomfortable experience I had of the three and a half years that I was in nursing school. I was too young and emotionally inexperienced to deal with such a serious situation.

My feelings were mixed. I had to follow doctor's orders that went against my inclination: to force feed a seriously sick and helpless patient that I thought bordered on cruel treatment. If I refused to follow the orders of my superiors, I would be summarily kicked out of nursing school.

On the third day Doctor Miller walked into the room while I was struggling to feed Mrs. Botha.

"Stop!" he said. "It's no use going on like this."

I don't know if it was only then that he realized what drastic measures we had to take to follow his orders. Instead of helping a patient we caused pain and suffering. Intravenous feeding that could make life easier for patients and staff alike was still far in the future.

"We might as well give up," he said with some sadness. "I think she's not going to live much longer."

He predicted right. That evening Mrs. Botha mercifully slipped into a coma, and a few days later, with her children at her bedside, her wish to die was fulfilled. I was relieved that Mrs. Botha's life had come to an end, and that she was finally at peace. But the feelings of guilt I felt then in my share of not understanding

Travelling Beyond Borders

and sympathizing more with a patient's wish to die, even if it was not legally possible, still remain.

In our senior year we had to go through training for night duty, meaning work at night and sleep by day, for a month. It took some time for the body to adjust to this new rhythm (called Circadian rhythm). There was only an hour's break to eat dinner around midnight. We had to check in at six pm so that the day staff could go over every patient's chart with us to note changes and medication.

There were only two of us who worked in a ward. A senior nurse sat in a small office where we could call her if there was a problem. We took turns every hour to go around the ward to check on every patient to make sure they were okay, and dispense medication where needed. At seven am, the next morning we followed the same routine of going over every patient's chart. At the end of the month we got two days off, usually over the weekend, so that our bodies could adjust to the regular Circadian rhythm again.

Night duty did not come without an occasional drama. When it was my turn to do night duty, my co-worker, Nancy, and I were assigned to the woman's medical ward. When we checked in at six pm one day, the head nurse of the day team told us that a new patient, Mrs. Taylor, had been admitted earlier in the afternoon after she suffered a mild heart attack at home. She was put into a small room with just one other patient close to the nurses station where we could keep an eye on her.

As always, patients were put into bed in an upright position with some extra pillows to make resting and sleeping easier. Mrs Taylor was a friendly, overweight eighty-year-old woman. who seemed less anxious after she was admimitted and given medication to relieve chest pain. During the night we took turns to check on all patients. Around ten pm it was my turn. I checked on Mrs Taylor who seemed to be sleeping peacefully. An hour later Nancy went to check on Mrs Taylor. She barely entered the room when she rushed out with a look of horror on her face and unable to speak. She just pointed to the room then sat down and cried hysterically.

I went to the room and saw that Mrs Taylor had apparently died.

Her upper false teeth had slipped out of her mouth and landed on her chin which, in the half dark, had the semblance of an evil ghoulish grin. I understood the reason for Nancy's horror.

I called the night nurse and she in turn called the in-house doctor to confirm Mrs.Taylor's death. He also called her family to tell them that their mother had died. The next day I heard that Nancy had quit nursing school and was already on her way home to her parents.

The Andrew McCollum Training Hospital did not have an Emergency Unit. For that we student nurses had to go to Pretoria's much larger General Hospital where we did a month long stint, and living in a temporary dorm on the Hospital premises.

There was also a separate Isolation building where we learned to care for patients who suffered from tropical and other infectious diseases. It was a small one story building that could only take in about twenty patients. Each patient was put in a cubicle size room with one window that overlooked a beautiful garden with shady trees, and a variety of flowers. It was peaceful and quiet there, screened from the continuous noisy bustle of the General Hospital in the distance.

Some of the patients were children. For them, especially the small ones, being isolated with no parents allowed to visit, bordered on a traumatic experience.

All they saw every day were people who were dressed in white gowns and boots, their smiles hidden behind a mask. I learned then to talk in a cheerful but soothing voice. We also encouraged parents to bring a favorite toy. It was only much later that we realized that bringing a favorite toy was a mistake because when the children were discharged, they had to leave the toy behind as it was

Travelling Beyond Borders

considered contaminated. So, from then on it was to bring a toy they had no problem leaving behind.

For the less sick, I pointed out the beautiful garden and asked them to see how many birds they could see hopping from branch to branch on the trees. This was my effort at keeping their minds off from feeling isolated. It did not always work, but I learned a lot about patient care at that time.

There was a laundry room and separate kitchen to prepare food for the patients. We had to wear protective gowns, cloth boots, and masks when we went into their rooms to wash them, change the sheets, or brought them warmed up sterilized bed pans. When a patient had recovered enough to go home, they were taken to a special shower room close to the back door. After a shower the patient had to go into a small room to change into clothing that the family had brought along, and then go outside. They were not allowed back in. Working in the Isolation building was important training, but of all the classes I found it the most boring.

Most of the excitement and drama happened in Emergency. We treated anything from heart attacks, suicide attempts, severe burns, broken bones, bullet wounds, to coughs, sniffles, and sore heads.

Early one afternoon a young man brought in a woman who sobbed uncontrollably, holding a small folded towel over her chest and in obvious pain. After I admitted her, I took her to a private cubicle and examined her chest. She was bleeding from her left breast where her nipple was supposed to be. I also had to ask questions so that I could report to the attending doctor. How did the injury happen? The woman, unable to answer, just sobbed. I asked the young man if he could tell me.

He turned red in the face with embarrassment. "It was an accident," he said nervously. "I . . . I . . . bit it off."

I didn't understand. "How?" I asked.

"When we were having sex," he whispered.

When the doctor walked in, he asked the man to wait outside while he examined the patient. I reported to him what the young man had told me.

"I see," the doctor said trying not to smile.

After examining her breast he said, "We will have to move you to the operating room and get you ready for surgery to repair the damage. I'll go and tell your husband."

The woman let out a wail. "He's not my husband! My husband is at work."

The doctor raised his eyebrows and said in a matter of fact way, "So that's how it is."

When we left the cubicle, he told the young man he was free to leave, and that he would call the woman's husband to let him know about the surgery. Shaking his head as we walked to the admitting desk, the doctor said, "You can bet there's going to be hell to pay when I call the husband to tell him his wife's in hospital for breast surgery, and why."

I just nodded, half stunned by what I had just witnessed. At the age of nineteen years I was still very naïve about passion and sexual relationships, but on that day I learned that adultery can sometimes ruin a woman or a man's life.

In the beginning of my senior year I was assigned to the women's surgical ward for a few months. One day a plain looking woman in her mid-forties was brought in to undergo a vaginal hysterectomy. The day after her admittance she had the surgery. Two days later she went home to recover from the surgery, which takes several weeks and without sexual activity. Two days later she was back in the surgical ward in bad shape, with severe bleeding from the vagina. The surgeon repaired the obvious damage.

I did not know how that happened. The poor woman was emotional and seemed very upset. I decided to ask her what happened. She started to sob, so I sat down by her bed, held her hand, and gently stroked her cheek.

Between sobs she said when she got home her husband raped her repeatedly.

Travelling Beyond Borders

The next morning after he left for work, she called her neighbor to come and help her move out of the house and take her to her sister who lived a few blocks away. Her sister called the surgeon, and he said she should bring the woman to the hospital immediately. The doctor was so furious with the husband that he reported him to the police. I don't remember what happened after that. The doctor later told me the woman ended up living with her sister, and filed for divorce. This is another instance of how we never know what happens in the privacy of homes: abusive husbands, child abuse, and so on.

The majority of doctors that I met did an excellent job of caring for their patients. Except one of them, Dr. Smith, who, with his odd behavior, made me wonder where he got his medical degree. I was in my senior year, and had to work in the men's medical ward to prepare for final exams. My job, among others, was to dispense medication, and give shots where needed.

Dr Smith's patient was an elderly man who needed a daily dose of four ounces of Vitamin K. This required a larger syringe, and longer needle, and had to be injected very slowly so that the liquid could be absorbed into the body. The natural sources of Vitamin K come from green leafy vegetables like kale, spinach, broccoli, and Brussels sprouts. Lesser sources come from fish, beef, dairy products, and some cereals. Vitamin K is a nutrient that the body needs to stay healthy. It's important for blood clotting, healthy bones, and also has other functions in the body.

One morning, just after I had given his patient his shot of Vitamin K, Dr. Smith walked into the room, followed by the head nurse. He asked me if I had given his patient the Vitamin K already.

I said yes and pointed to the empty syringe.

"I just cancelled the dose," he said and told me to withdraw the liquid.

I was puzzled, and did not know how to do it.

"Just put the needle back into the butt and withdraw it."

This made no sense. It's like pouring water into sand and there is no way you can get it back, but I tried, Nothing. He pointed to another area, still nothing.

He angrily grabbed the syringe out of my hand, saying "Nurse, you are so stupid," and plunged the needle in with such force that the patient moaned in pain.

No liquid came out.

The head nurse intervened, saying that since I did not know he had cancelled the shot that we could consider it as the last one. With obvious irritation he pulled out the syringe, threw it on the bed, and without saying goodbye to his patient, walked to the door, followed by the head nurse. When she came to the door she turned around and gave me a big smile and winked at me. I smiled back. This was the kind of humor bordering on comedy that you did not often experience in a hospital.

I graduated in early 1959 after almost four years in nursing school. Instead of attending the graduation ceremony, I walked down the isle of our local church on the same day to get married to my best friend, Hendrik Boers.

China Blue Cups

My mother loved antiques. Since my childhood anything from large pieces of ornate furniture to small objects eventually found their way to our house. And always I heard, "This will be yours one day," or "This will go to John—my brother—when I'm gone."

It was not only her love for beautiful things that fed her almost obsessive quest for antiques. She collected any old item; kitchen utensils, copper kettles, old coffee grinders, coal heated irons, dishes, painted teapots to the crocheted doilies of my grandmother, anything that reminded her of her childhood in Holland. She had through the years created her own Utopia of what her life in Holland would have been if she had not been forced at age fourteen to move with her family to settle on a farm in South Africa.

To make up for her loss she endeavored to create a Dutch atmosphere in our house. To do that, she had to persuade my father to give her the money to buy furniture, and other Dutch knickknacks. That was not always easy.

My father had a quirky way of making her feel inferior whenever she asked for money. It was *his* money, and she had to give him a good reason for wanting to buy "that old junk." The conversation often ended with my mother getting angry and sulking for the next few days.

Then, out of the blue, my father would casually tell her she could go ahead and buy what she wanted. It was to watch her delight and excitement that he was after. And when she had placed knickknacks and arranged the furniture just right, he praised her artistic talent for creating a *"gezellige koamer,"* a cozy room. I was getting ready for final exams at nursing school in Pretoria when I went home for a few days to plan the last details of my upcoming wedding in a few months. Instead of attending my graduation ceremony, February 28, 1959, I would walk down the isle of the church to get married.

When I came into the dining room, I saw a set of twelve antique China blue teacups, neatly arranged on the antique buffet.

I asked my mother where she got those exquisite hand painted cups.

"Oh, I didn't buy them," she said, "Oma Hommes sent them."

She pointed to a marble Victorian clock and two matching candelabra on the mantel piece, also from my grandmother.

It turned out that my grandmother—who lived in Holland—had sold her house, and moved into a retirement home. Most of the family heirlooms went to my father's oldest sister who lived in Amsterdam. The cups, clock, and a few other items were sent to my father.

"You will get these cups one day and John will get the clock and candelabra when I'm gone," my mother said. I was delighted and thanked her with a kiss.

Six months after our wedding my husband and I traveled to Germany where he studied for his PhD in Theology. After three and a half years we went home; my husband with a degree in his pocket, and I carrying our two-year-old daughter, Greta.

Several months later we packed up again to move to America where Hendrik was appointed as professor of New Testament Theology at Emory.

Our daughter Greta was about sixteen and her twin sisters ten years old when my mother called to say that my father's health had deteriorated and he was selling the farm. They planned to retire to a quiet neighborhood of Johannesburg. Would I like to come for a last visit to the farm? she asked. They would pay my airplane ticket. I jumped at the opportunity, and after making a series of "heat and eat" dishes for my family, I flew to South Africa.

It was a wonderful, memory filled two weeks and I thoroughly enjoyed the visit with my parents. The day before I was to fly back home, I walked into the living room for ten o'clock coffee. My parents were having a loud argument.

Travelling Beyond Borders

My father was sitting in his comfortable armchair, and I heard him shout, "I would have given John my father's gold watch on Ida's wedding day if you had given her the blue cups my mother sent as a wedding gift."

My mother was standing by the buffet in the adjoining dining room. Her cheeks were flushed red and in an angry voice she said, "Ida, do you want these cups?"

It was a very awkward moment. At first, I didn't know how to react, but finally, in a timid voice, I said, "Yes please, Mamma."

"Well take them then," she said and walked out of the room.

I sat down with my father, stunned by my mother's angry reaction to the embarrassment of being exposed for keeping what was not rightfully hers for so many years. I told him that I felt guilty and sad because I had never thanked my grandmother for her generous gift. It was too late now; she had died a few years earlier.

"Don't worry too much," he replied. "You know your mother; I think she thanked your Oma for them many years ago."

The next day peace was restored. I had carefully wrapped each cup and saucer in tissue paper and put them in a small box that I held on my lap during the seventeen hour flight back to Atlanta.

A month later a large box from South Africa was delivered at our house. In it was a replica of an antique Dutch wall cabinet with a note from my mother:

I had this cabinet made especially for you to hold your blue China cups.
                     With love, Mamma.

Wigboldus Homerus' Seals

Farm Schiedam, Gronigen, the Netherlands

Grietje Glas and Engel Engels Engagement

Grietje Engels and Ida Gezina Hommes

Ida and her Guardian Angel

Oberholzer Train Station,
Gauteng, South Africa

Hommes Family, Gronigen,
Jan Eggo Hommes (L)

Boerdery Hommes, Oberholzer, Gauteng

Jan Eggo and his little helper Ida

Jan Eggo, John, Gezina, and Ida

Ida and Lisa wash clothes

Schapara. I. *Smearing a courtyard floor, 1953, The Bantu-speaking Tribes of South Africa*. Cape Town, South Africa: Maskew Miller Limited.

Lisa, Ida and Saara

Tidda and Saara

Ida in her high school uniform

Dominee Beyers Naude
(Dutch National Archives CC 3.0 NL)

Friends at University of Pretoria

Nurse Ida, R.N.

Friends at Andrew McColm
Training Hospital

Section IV:
Memories of WWII

Childhood Memories of World War II

Three Blue Plates

Four Women and War

Code Name "Big Cat"

Childhood Memories of World War Two

After I finished reading Cornelius Ryan's book *The Longest Day* earlier this year, I was interested in reading more about the history of WWII.

I found two books that previously belonged to my father: *Ambassador Dodd's Diary 1933–1938*, and *Berlin Diary* by William L. Shirer. Instead of my father's forceful signature with which he claimed ownership of every book in his library, I saw another name: Dr. Hanne Zeehoff, Stinkhoutboom (Stinkwood tree) Farm, P.O. Box, Oberholzer, TVL, S.A. (Transvaal, South Africa.) Underneath it I saw my own attempts at writing—signing my name with curly loops and the number 5 filling the page; the age I was then.

The name Hanne Zeehoff brought back memories of my childhood during the war years and how it affected the small community of Dutch farmers from Holland who—encouraged and sponsored by the South African government—came to settle in Oberholzer in 1928 and later.

Most of them—among them my father and my mother with her family—came from the Provence of Groningen where the Eems River, flowing lazily towards the North Sea, forms the northern border between Holland and Germany.

The Dutch farmers moved from a compact country with too much water to settle in a country where water had to be pumped from an underground lake and an occasional thunderstorm was considered a gift from heaven.

They left behind family, friends and farms that had been plowed for centuries, to create new farms on the spacious uncultivated Transvaal veldt.

But while the Dutch farmers were creating a new life for themselves in South Africa, they remained emotionally attached to their mother country. They socialized only with their kind, conversed in the Groninger dialect that had its roots in 15th century Saxon—in contrast to the locals who spoke Afrikaans, a new language that evolved in the early 18th century mostly from Dutch with some French, German, and Malay mixed in.

They hoisted the Dutch flag on the roof of a new-built house, not the South African one, and on festive occasions sang the Dutch national anthem "*Wilhelmus*," not "God save the King"—all of which did not sit too well with the local residents who considered the "Hollanders" as "foreign invaders of our land."

One family, Lotte and Wilhelm Steinthal and Lotte's widowed mother, Dr. Hanne Zeehoff, a medical doctor, did not seem to fit in with any other group in our community. They were Jews from Manheim who fled Nazi Germany in the mid-thirties, leaving the rest of their relatives behind. That they were from a wealthy and cultured upper class was obvious when they brought along a shipload of antique furniture and enough money to buy a large, abandoned farm with two houses on it that were completely renovated before they moved in. (Why they chose to live in such a remote, God-forsaken area was never revealed.)

The farm that the Steinthals and Hanne Zeehoff bought was about five miles west of ours. It was formerly owned by a member of a wealthy Afrikaner family, the Oberholzers—that gave their name to the community—who settled there before the Anglo-Boer War (1899–1902).

The Oberholzers, like the majority of Afrikaner farmers—or "The Boers" as they were known to the outside world—not only lost the war against Britain, they also lost everything they owned when British soldiers slaughtered their cattle, burnt their crops and carted their wives and children to concentration camps where many died of starvation and disease, leaving a proud Afrikaner nation embittered, with a hatred of anything British, and reduced to second class citizens in their own country which was now part of the British Empire.

My parents soon befriended the Steinthals and Hanne Zeehoff, all three fluent in English. My father, the only one with a college degree in our Dutch community, who frequently went on cultural tours all over Germany as a young man, found like-minded friends who could talk about Old Europe and the current political situation. My mother went to drink afternoon tea with Lotte or Hanne, mainly to admire, and covet, the beautiful family heirlooms—some dating back to the 17th century—that were so artistically displayed in the Steinthal and Zeehoff' houses.

I was always eager to go with my mother especially when she visited Hanne or "Tante Hanne" (Tante = aunt) as I was told to call her. It wasn't Tante Hanne, a tiny sad looking woman, that made me eager to go along; it was her bathroom that fascinated me. It was like no other bathroom I had ever seen. The walls were covered with sparkling white tiles with black trim and the floor with alternating black and white. In our bathroom the cement walls and floor were painted a hideous apple green. Hanne's bathroom had a flush toilet; we still used a smelly outhouse.

What interested me was a mysterious silver colored gadget above the two faucets of the bathtub that rested on a cradle like a telephone without the mouthpiece. I picked it up and held the top part to my ear and my imagination instantly transformed the gadget into a telephone. From then on, every time we visited Hanne, I sat on the toilet next to the bathtub and had long conversations with an imaginary friend on my "telephone." Until one day when Tante Hanne walked into the bathroom and showed me how a handheld shower was used. That somehow broke the spell and I never played in the bathroom again.

The last Dutch couple to move into our community were Mr. Kerling and his wife, both teachers, who hailed from Amsterdam.

Mr. Kerling was appointed principal of the small two room school with a corrugated iron roof and a fenced in yard that kept wandering cows from the neighboring farm out, and the children in. A shabbily constructed outhouse stood in a corner close to the fence.

I met Master Kerling when I entered first grade in 1942. Grey-haired and dapper, he strutted about, proudly surveying his small domain of school yard and outhouse as if he were the executive of a large company. He was obviously fond of children, strict but kind, and passionately dedicated to their education.

The Kerlings did not mix with our Groninger community. He was an educated man while most of the farmers had barley made it through high school and talked only of their crops and cattle. Instead, Mr. Kerling immersed himself in the Afrikaner Cause: from their culture to their politics, including a shared hatred of the British. Why, remains a mystery, but how much, came to light several years later.

In the early morning hours of May 10th, 1940—a glorious spring day in Holland when apple trees were blossoming and vast tulip fields were in full bloom—a swarm of Hitler's planes loaded with bombs, flew across the German border into Groningen and headed southward.

A mere seven kilometers into Groningen the planes flew over the 200-year-old family farm where my father grew up and learned to milk a cow as a little boy and to plow the land with a new tractor, the year before he moved to South Africa in 1928. Then to the nearby village of Beerta, where he went to school, and the clock in the church tower solemnly tolled the early morning hour six times as they flew over.

Ten kilometers further on the planes reached the farm where my mother was born and where she and her siblings walked to school in the nearby town of Noordbroek. On their way, passing a majestic 13th century church that towered over the town and surrounding Groninger landscape, unaware that my mother's ancestor, Ellery Eppens, pastor from 1625 till his death in 1672, lay buried under the church floor, close to the pulpit.

Hitler's planes droned over peaceful farmlands where farmers were planting summer crops, over villages with slow spinning windmills and medieval towns with narrow streets. And all along their flight southward the unsuspecting Dutch people looked to the sky and wondered and asked, "Where do those many planes come from? Where are they headed?"

Travelling Beyond Borders

The harbor city of Rotterdam, at the other end of Holland, is where those planes were headed. There their bombs rained down, and in a matter of minutes killed over a thousand civilians and destroyed a city that was already more than a century old when Desiderius Erasmus, Erasmus of Rotterdam, renowned Dutch Theologian and Philosopher, was born in 1466.

And so began the war for the peace loving Dutch people and five years of tyrannical Nazi occupation.

Later that same day in South Africa, my father turned on the radio and heard the deep voice of the announcer saying "This is BBC news from London," followed by the stunning news that Holland had been invaded by Germany and Hitler's triumphant proclamation that Holland was now part of the Third Reich in order to protect the Dutch from the war-mongering British!

I was barely four years old then, and unaware of the unfolding drama till my mother said, "You can't play the piano today,"—loudly banging the keys, mimicking my father's way of playing Beethoven—"You have to be very quiet because Pappa wants to listen to the news."

If I sat quietly, she said, I would hear the sound of planes flying over London. Which of course, I never did. I didn't understand much of what was going on, but that something bad was happening in Holland and other countries far away became clear by the somber look on my father's face as he leaned over the armrest of his Morris chair with his ear close to the little radio to catch every word of the latest news.

The German invasion of Holland affected everyone in our community. The worst was the loss of all communication with our families. Holland was in chaos. Letters and news to and from the outside world were restricted and censored. It was late August before my father got a letter from his parents to say that a telegram announcing the birth of my brother on June 15th had finally reached them.

For the Steinthals and Hanne the invasion of Holland spelled personal disaster. They had no doubt that any of their relatives who managed to flee Germany and found refuge in Holland, Belgium and France were eventually going to be rounded up by the Gestapo and end up in concentration camps.

Other than the gloomy daily news of the war in faraway Europe, life on the farm went on as before: the cows were milked, crops were planted and harvested, and the bright sun came up every day and went down again on our peaceful farm.

I learned about the war through Life Magazine that regularly arrived in the mail. Photos of planes on fire falling from the sky into the sea, sinking warships; smoke rising from bombed cities; bodies of dead American soldiers on a beach, alternated with advertisements of "Formfit" Woman's Underwear; Kolynos Tooth Powder; Rice Krispies Cereal; the latest model Packard cars and Camel cigarettes. I looked at them all with equal interest without comprehending the horror of war.

Some changes in our daily life were inevitable as the war raged on in Europe. One day my mother announced that from now on we would only get brown bread instead of white.

My brother and I protested loudly but my mother just said, "There is a war going on and we have to do our share to help the fighting soldiers. Besides, brown bread is good for you."

Only years later did we find out that while we were grumbling about having to eat brown bread—spread thickly with homemade butter and jam—our cousins in Holland, where food was rationed, often went hungry and were limited to one egg a week and one slice of dry bread per day, sometimes spread with a tablespoon of syrup if they were lucky, while we had fresh eggs and milk every day.

In early 1944 Master Kerling, the school principal, suddenly disappeared. No one knew where he was. I was in a different school five miles away by then and unaware of his disappearance. A few weeks later came the shocking news. Mr. Kerling and a group of Afrikaner men had been arrested and jailed for sabotage!

My father told me the story several years later. When the war broke out in 1940, Mr. Kerling joined an underground group called Die Afrikaner Broederbond (The Afrikaner Brotherhood), who, in sympathy with the German cause, were bent on sabotaging the South African-British war effort: anything from cutting telephone lines, stealing gasoline—to prevent trucks from transporting goods to the harbors—to blowing up railway lines. How much damage they did was known only to the secret police.

The allied invasion of Normandy on June 6th, 1944—so vividly portrayed in Cornelius Ryan's book—was the beginning of the end for Hitler's devastating war in Europe and his Third Reich. For the Dutch people five years of shackled Nazi occupation came to an end on May 5th, 1945.

When the news reached the Dutch community in South Africa they got together, raised a glass, and sang the Dutch national anthem in celebration.

The euphoria did not last long, reality and grieving soon took its place. Newspapers and hastily printed books brought home the horrible devastation in Europe. I was about ten when several books arrived at our house. One book had gruesome photos of ovens in concentration camps with burned bodies still visible and skeletal bodies of Jews stacked like cordwood ready for mass burial, images I can still recall to this day.

And then there was the incredible story of my father's best friend in high school, exposed as an enthusiastic Nazi supporter and special agent for the Gestapo in Groningen. He and his fellow traitors hunted down, and arrested hundreds of men and women of the underground resistance movement—most of whom were either promptly executed without trial or tortured to death.

Our family lost two family members in Groningen. One, an uncle of my mother who was summarily executed by a Gestapo officer in 1944 on his farm, in the presence of his family, for providing food to a family nearby who were hiding three Jews in their attic. The other, a cousin who was shot by a sniper while riding his bicycle the day after peace was declared.

For the Steinthals and Hanne the end of the war brought no consolation. Their entire family in Germany was wiped out. All of them ended up in the gas chambers. But a ray of hope appeared in their dark world. In late 1945, Lotte, Hanne's only child, gave birth to a baby boy. They named him Ivan, after Lotte's father.

In 1946 I entered fourth grade in a new school three miles from our farm. The principal was none other than Mr. Kerling, back in circulation after almost two years in jail, and no sign of embarrassment or regret for his traitorous crimes. He was the same Master Kerling I met in first grade: cheerfully welcoming the pupils back to school. And this time he had a real reason to strut about and survey his domain: a brick building with five classrooms connected by a porch, separate bathrooms for boys and girls and a fence around the playground to keep us safe, not from wandering cows but traffic passing by.

Five long years of war had come to an end and life in our community continued its normal peaceful pace with no more worries about our families in Holland. And the best was that my brother and I were allowed to eat white bread again.

Three Blue Plates

A Personal Story of WWII

While I was cleaning my bookshelves and looking through my collection of books I found Albert Speer's memoir *Inside the Third Reich*, a fascinating description of his close association with Hitler, first as his architect, later as his Minister of Armaments.

Rereading the book, I was struck once again of how one man, Adolf Hitler, managed to destroy the lives of millions of people all over the world.

One quiet afternoon, in the summer of 1994 when I was about halfway through the book, the phone suddenly rang. It was my cousin calling from Groningen in Holland. Her father, Wieto Meiborg, had died on June 22, in the same town, Scheemda, where he was born, 92 years before.

Uncle Wieto was one of my favorite uncles and I was sad to hear of his death, but consoled by so many fond memories I could look back on.

I got to know him and my aunt Rienie, my mother's cousin, really well when my mother and I went to Groningen in 1984 and spent three weeks with them. Their house was dollhouse small but the warmth, good humor and hospitality enveloped us more than made up for its size.

A proud Groninger, Uncle Wieto relished the sound of the dialect as he spoke it, telling stories and typical Groninger jokes, and writing poetry that portrayed the humor and oddities of his fellow Groningers.

We shared an interest in genealogy. He was the first to guide me through the process of putting all the information into the computer. We traveled through the Groninger countryside to visit farms where my ancestors worked the land centuries ago, the churches they attended and the cemeteries where they were buried.

For Uncle Wieto it was also an opportunity to show me and my mother around his beloved Groningen—anything beyond its borders was "Holland" to him, almost like a foreign country. We drove by fields of ripening wheat; along water canals where sheep grazed; passed through small centuries old towns; on to where house high dikes protected the land from the ever threatening flooding of the North Sea; ate freshly caught fish in a room size restaurant sitting on top of a dike.

On one of these trips when we were about half a mile from Scheemda where he lived, he stopped in front of an impressive three story house, almost Victorian in style and unusual for the region, but with the typical large barn attached at the back like all other farmhouses in Groningen.

"This is the farm where I grew up," he said. "You see all that land behind the barn? I plowed and planted it with my father since I was a teenager."

"When I was doing genealogy research," he went on, "I discovered that the farm dates back to 1598 but it only came into our family in 1890."

He pointed to the house. "My grandfather built it in 1912 when he inherited the farm from my great-grandfather. And when my grandfather died my father got it."

The house was built with the best materials available at that time, and the barn completely renovated, all for 54000 guilders. In today's evaluation that would translate into about two million dollars, more than most people could afford.

It didn't occur to me then to ask why he, the only son, wasn't still living and working on the farm. But, purely by chance and in an unexpected way, I soon heard how it happened.

I was standing in their small hallway one morning admiring three hand painted blue plates hanging on the wall, when my aunt walked by. I asked her about them.

"Ask your uncle," she said, "he'll tell you the story."

"Those plates belonged to my mother," Uncle Wieto began his story.

"They were part of her dowry of old family heirlooms including furniture that she brought to the house when she married my father."

"My mother died when I was seventeen years old. Two years later my father married the housekeeper. I don't know what my father saw in her. She was a dour woman with no sense of humor. But she cooked and cleaned and provided comfort in bed I guess," he said with a wry smile. "A few years later she had a baby girl and life went on."

That peaceful life came to a dramatic end on May 10th, 1940, when a stunned Dutch nation watched Hitler's air force and army invade their country.

With it came Hitler's message to the Dutch. "We are not taking over your country. We have come to protect you from the war mongering British."

"That so called *protection*," Uncle Wieto continued, "turned out to be a gradual enslavement of the Dutch people. They soon sent out long lists of orders such as, turn in our radios. The reason? so that we couldn't listen to the British BBC News propaganda against the peace loving Germans.

"Then two more ominous orders were issued. First a curfew: all Jews to be off the streets by seven pm every evening and second: all Jews, including children over the age of five are to wear a gold colored star on their chests. This made it easier to round them up and take truckloads of them to . . . where? We didn't know till much later. A place called Westerbork."

The Westerbork camp was created by Dutch authorities in 1939 as a temporary safe haven for the thousands of Jews who fled Nazi Germany. But in an ironic twist of fate the Germans took over the camp in 1942 and turned it into a concentration camp from where Jews and other "Enemies of the Reich" were taken to extermination camps in Germany and Poland.

All these orders were issued by German officials who took over the running of local governments and police stations. Seeing that the orders were carried out however was done by local Dutch Nazi Party members, the NSB-ers as they were called, and despised by their fellow citizens. Many of them had a criminal background, and though the German officials had no respect for them, they were very convenient to do their dirty work.

By 1943 an order for the Dutch to turn in their bicycles came directly from Albert Speer, by then the Minister of Armaments who was in dire need of any metal for his weapons factories. This was a major blow for the bicycle riding Dutch. Many refused and were summarily arrested and put in jail.

"We also got that order," Uncle Wieto went on," but first I have to tell you about my father."

"My father was a clever and well educated man, but a bit rough in his ways. A don't-mess-with-me, I-rule-here type. When he got word to turn in his bicycle he just exploded. 'Not going to,' was all he said. Instead we made a tunnel inside the stacks of baled hay in the barn and hid all our bicycles there. Nobody ever found them.

"My father was a good man. For almost a year he took milk, eggs and whatever food he could gather—food was getting scarce by then because most of what we produced was sent to Germany—to a house about a mile from our farm. He never told us, and we never asked who the food was for.

"Then, on September 20th, 1944—I will never forget that day—we found out. Two of those Dutch NSB-ers—damn bastards!—appeared behind the barn where my father and I were shoveling cow dung onto the compost heap. They had orders to arrest him, one of them said, for not turning in his bicycle and for aiding Jews by supplying them with food.

"For a long time they had secretly watched my father's every move and became suspicious about the house he visited so often. They discovered three Jews in the attic, hidden behind a cleverly built wall. The Dutch couple who hid them was also arrested."

"'They're on their way to the concentration camp right now,' one of them said with a triumphant look on his face. Then he pointed a finger at my father, 'And you're next!'

"The sight of this scrawny, cocky, barely out of his teens, kid ordering him around was too much for my father. He lifted his spade in the air as if to strike and roared, 'Get off my property you traitorous scrap of dirt! Or I'll use this on you,' raising the shovel higher."

"The two walked off in a great hurry with a 'Just wait Meiborg. We'll get you still!'

"Early the next morning, my stepmother appeared behind the barn where my father and I were cleaning up the stable. With her were the same scrawny kid and two Germans armed with pistols of the so-called Homeland Defense Front, also known as the Gestapo.

"One of them, speaking in German, said 'Meiborg, we've had an official report that you resisted arrest for crimes you committed: one: not turning in your bicycles, two: aiding the Enemy of the Reich (Jews), and three: threatening the lives of our officials with a dangerous weapon.'

"Without warning he pulled out his gun and shot my father between the eyes. As they walked away that little NSB-er bastard looked at me with an evil grin on his face, 'Bury him in that pile of dung, where he belongs.'"

Uncle Wieto choked back tears, unable to continue. Telling the story—maybe for the first time—brought back a too vivid memory of his father's execution.

After a while he continued his story of what happened next.

"Soon after my father's death, we were informed that he had left no will. According to inheritance law, the farm, the house and contents—all my mother's family heirlooms too—now belonged to my stepmother.

"I was penniless; reduced to an ordinary farmhand on my father's farm. That was the offer from my stepmother: I could earn my keep as a laborer. I had nowhere else to go so I stayed."

On May 8th, 1945, just eight months after this tragic incident, Canadian soldiers crossed the borders into the Netherlands and the Dutch were freed from five years of hellish Nazi tyranny.

Uncle Wieto was almost done with his story.

"A year after the war ended, I married my high school sweetheart, your Aunt Rienie. She's been the best partner any man could wish for. I was still working on the farm and we lived in a small apartment inside the barn, where the farmhands used to live."

He laughed, shaking his head at the irony of it all. "And my stepmother lived in that big house by herself with her daughter."

"But things got better," he continued. "After two years of working as a farm laborer for a mere pittance, your aunt Rienie inherited enough money from her father in 1948, which allowed us to buy this house and a tractor for me. I rented myself and my tractor out to local farmers to plow their lands and plant crops. It was seasonal work which suited me well.

"Several years later, in 1953, my stepmother called me in and told me she was going to sell the farm and everything on it: cattle, farm implements—the whole lot, including everything in the house. She was tired of coping with all the work on the farm, she said. And besides, she needed the money.

"I asked her if I could have a few things that belonged to my mother. 'Like what?' she asked. I didn't know; there were so many things that reminded me of my mother but I finally picked the three blue plates.

"She showed no sign of empathy or even understanding of what all this meant to me. 'You can have them if you pay for them,' she said.

"And that's how I got those blue plates."

NOTE:

When the contents of the house went on sale, my uncle and aunt went back to the house and bought a small desk that belonged to Uncle Wieto's father, a corner cabinet to display some old dinner dishes that belonged to his mother and an ornate rocking chair, also from her dowry. Their house was so small that they could not fit in other pieces of furniture, but they were happy with what they got.

Four Women and a War

Germany, 1959

Adelheid and Marianne Blum

"I found us another, bigger place," my husband, Hendrik, said when he walked into our matchbox-size attic apartment. The small two story house in Ippendorf where we had moved in just a month before belonged to two sisters, Adelheid and Marianne Blum.

Soon after we moved in they invited us for a cup of get-acquainted coffee. All they knew was that we were from South Africa and that Hendrik had received a study grant from the Alexander von Humboldt Foundation, sponsored by the German government.

The sisters told us their story. Before the war they were members of a traveling circus. Adelheid—married with two children—was a trapeze artist and Marianne, a ballerina, danced on running horses. Their mother was Jewish.

Their father, accused of being a "Jewish Sympathizer," was transported with his family to a concentration camp by the Nazis. They and their father were the only survivors. The rest of the family, including Adelheid's children, five and seven, died of starvation and typhus.

After the war the German government compensated them for all they had lost. With the money they bought the house, conveniently close to Bonn, the capital of West Germany at that time. By renting out the furnished first floor and the attic to foreigners they hoped to supplement their meager income.

The sisters were understandably upset by our planned move. We were sad too because we liked the two friendly women. We explained that the other apartment had bigger rooms and central heating, for the same price. Their attic apartment was unheated except for a small stove in the living room. Winter was on the way and with only one blanket on the bed, we had to move. With a limited budget, we could not afford extra blankets.

When the sisters couldn't persuade us to stay their friendliness turned to hostility. There was no doubt, they said, that it was their Jewish background that had influenced our decision to leave. After all, we came from the "Land of Apartheid." It wasn't true of course, but when they refused to even say goodbye, we left with sadness and a great deal of guilt.

Fraulein Traude Pungs and Frau Hilde Ziegler.

Fraulein Pungs owned a large three story house in the quiet neighborhood of Bad-Godesberg, a suburb of Bonn, where embassies, consulates, and diplomats from a variety of countries were housed in elegant old mansions. A short way down the street was the Rhine River. It was the ideal place to go for walks or sit on a bench and watch the traffic of international barges chugging by. It would be our home for the next two years.

The first thing we saw when we entered the house were four pairs of old fashioned shoes neatly arranged under the coat rack in the hallway. They belonged to Fraulein Pungs, and there was a story behind those shoes.

We shared the second floor with Frau Ziegler who had made a one-room home for herself in the biggest bedroom. We shared the toilet on the landing with her and a young couple who lived upstairs on the third floor.

Our apartment consisted of a bedroom and a sitting room with balcony. Adjacent to it was a large bathroom. In a niche of the bathroom stood a stove, storage cupboard and small kitchen sink. A table and two chairs was wedged between the bathtub and wash basin. We were happy.

Shortly after we moved in, Fraulein Pungs invited us for a glass of wine to get acquainted. She told us her story.

Her parents were German but the family lived near Brussels in Belgium. Their father was a wealthy industrialist and she and her brother grew up in a large mansion surrounded by a park. A horde of servants took care of all their needs and served meals wearing white gloves. They had private tutors who saw to their education.

Then WW1 broke out. Her father's factory was confiscated, lost most of his money, and was deported back to Germany with the family. What little money was left was used to buy the house where she now lived. Adjusting to a life without luxuries and servants was difficult. Their mother had a nervous breakdown and became an invalid.

Soon after they moved in, Traude's father called her into the living room and pointed to four pairs of shoes he had bought. "These are for you," he said. The sturdiest pair were for working in the garden and mowing the grass. Another pair was for working inside the house, cooking, and cleaning. The next pair for walks outdoors and the best pair for going out.

Traude, barely twenty years old, heard with shock what was expected of her. But she pulled through and by the time WWII broke out—and her parents were no longer living—she had learned to take care of herself. Just like the Blum sisters, she had to rent out rooms to supplement her income. By then the first four pairs of shoes were replaced by a series of new ones that lasted through the 2nd war and were still in use when we moved in.

We soon realized that the shoes also sent a "message." If the first pair was missing, she was in the garden; the second pair that she was in the house somewhere, the third that she was out shopping and the fourth that she was visiting friends, usually on Sundays.

In time we heard Frau Ziegler's story too. A soft spoken, emotionally fragile woman, we never heard her laugh in the two years we lived there. She lost everything in the war. Her husband, a soldier, killed on the battlefield two months into the war. Her house was completely destroyed during a bombing raid. Her only child, a young man of 22 years, gunned down by a sniper three days after peace was declared.

As newcomers to Europe, my husband and I had to make adjustments too. Our country's racial policy was often the topic of conversation. We naively tried to explain the situation, mostly without success. Even Fraulein Pungs attacked us one day during a visit.

"How can you call yourself Christians when such horrible things take place in your country?"

By then we knew that no explanation would help. At some point Hendrik brought up the "Jewish Question." Pungs dismissed him with a shrug saying, "We didn't know." The standard answer most Germans came up with after the war.

Two years later Hendrik had a PhD in his pocket and we were ready to return to South Africa. Fraulein Pungs had advertised our apartment long before that.

One morning, on our way out we saw a tall well-dressed dark-skinned man on the doorstep. He was from Egypt and interested in renting the apartment. The Egyptian consulate was nearby. Fraulein Pungs invited him in. When we returned, we were eager to hear how the interview went. To our utter surprise she said, "I told the man the apartment wasn't available. I don't want such people in my house. I don't trust them."

Code Name: "Big Cat"

"How will I recognize him?" the undercover agent asked.

"He's about five eight, broad shouldered, with curly brown hair. You'll recognize him by the way he walks. Determined, focused. Like a big jungle cat with a limp stalking his prey," the CIA official replied. "That's why his code name is "Big Cat."

"What else?" the undercover agent asked.

"He's Jewish, but doesn't look Jewish. Born in Latvia. Grew up in Vienna where his parents settled before the first world war. He speaks German with a typical Austrian accent. Speaks French like a Frenchman, is fluent in English and knows his way around in all three countries."

"Your report says that he fled to France after Hitler invaded Austria. Is that correct?"

"Actually, he managed to escape from a prison six months after the Gestapo arrested him in Vienna."

"Why was he arrested?"

"He was suspected of working closely with Otto Von Hapsburg, who escaped to England some time ago, and with other members of the Imperial family's underground movement against the Anschluss (Annexation). Hitler wants to hunt them down and eliminate the lot of them. Two Hapsburg cousins are already in a concentration camp."

"What's 'Big Cat' doing in France now?"

"He joined the French underground resistance operated by the CIA, but we lost contact with him. We know the Gestapo spies are searching for him. That limp, the result of torture in prison, is a dead giveaway, and his life may be in danger. CIA headquarters wants you to track him down and get him to England as soon as possible. He can be of infinite help to us in decoding enemy messages. We think he's in the environs of Paris. When you find him use our secret code to identify yourself. Send a wire when you are ready."

A week later a coded wire reached CIA headquarters in New York: "Fish under water has crossed the pond."

This piece is based on a true story; told to me by "Big Cat" himself.

NOTE:

Big Cat's real name was Gregor Sebba. He became a faculty member of the ILA (Institute of Liberal Arts) at Emory in 1960 which was established in 1952. He earned two doctoral degrees while he was a student in Vienna: one in Economics and another in Political Science. While there he also made copies of original death masks of famous composers: Anton Bruckner, Beethoven, Gustav Mahler, and Franz List. And he also copied a death mask of the famous Russian ballerina Anna Pavlova, who became famous when she danced "The Dying Swan" of composer Peter Tchaikovsky's *Swan Lake*. These are now all in my house.

He was the most talented man I ever met. He taught Renaissance Art, the poetry of Rainier Maria Rilke, and wrote several books: *Life and Art of Alfred Kubin; The Dream of Descartes*, about the French Philosopher; *Creativity Lectures*, collected essays edited by Helen Sebba and Hendrikus Boers. Many of his papers are housed in the Emory Archives. He died in 1985.

Section V: From Marriage to the United States

The Proposal

The Irony of Apartheid

Welcome to America

A Radio Interview Brings Back Memories

The Proposal

"You're not my type," I told my future husband, soon after we first met. I was eighteen, a first year student at the University of Pretoria and trying to act mature and dignified. Hendrik was 27, with two degrees behind him, working on his Master's in Philosophy and plans for a PhD after that. I was intimidated by this talented man, but determined not to show it.

"So who's your type?" he wanted to know.

"My type is tall, handsome, Celtic type. A Scotsman who owns an old castle high on a mountain that overlooks the moors," I said dramatically, oblivious that I was exposing my girlish naiveté and unrealistic dreams of the ideal man. Hendrik was short and not very handsome.

He laughed heartily and wished me luck in finding such a Scotsman. The fool, he assured me with some irony, would get lost if he ever set foot outside Scotland, let alone find his way to South Africa.

We were drinking coffee and talking in his bed-sitting room of a Singles Only boarding house where I also rented a room at the opposite end of the hallway. There was no hint of romance or love in the air; we were just getting to know each other. All we had in common was that we both grew up on a farm, and shared a love of nature. We were opposites in just about everything else that mattered to us.

I loved dancing; he had no sense of rhythm and stumbled over his own feet when he tried. I loved movies; he considered them a waste of time. I wasn't very neat, except with my personal appearance; he had a finicky way of arranging things just so: the coffee cups on the serving tray always on the right, the sugar bowl always on the left, and his books in a straight line.

We both liked music. I watched with amazement how he built his own Hi-Fi system from scratch: carefully soldering hundreds of little wires together with a soldering iron, so that he could listen to his favorite classical music. I loved dance music, and knew all the latest pop songs by heart. He listened with a pained, lord-what-have-we-here look on his face, when I entertained him with my rendition of "On Top of Old Smokey."

Beethoven triggered the first real fight in our budding friendship. I told him I didn't like Beethoven: too loud and bombastic for my taste. He didn't talk to me for three days.

On the fourth day, when we accidentally met in the hallway, he greeted me with, "So, fat face, how are you?"

For some odd reason the words "fat face" sounded more like endearment than insult and made me happy.

In literature too, we had our differences. I liked Jane Austen. Romantic fluff he called it and not his kind of books. "Read Dostoevsky, that's where you find life in the raw," then went on to tell the story of Sonia in *Crime and Punishment*, breaking down and sobbing by the time he got the part where Sonia had sold her body for money to give to her poor parents.

I had never seen a grown man cry and felt embarrassed by this spectacle. I always thought a tough man didn't cry but, on that day, I learned that a man with empathy could.

By the end of the year we both knew that there was more than friendship between us. But Hendrik was clueless in the art of courtship. He hinted at a future life together but was in no hurry to get married.

Everything was put on hold when he went to Switzerland for six months to study at the International Institute de Bossey near Celigny. We wrote many letters: I wrote about nursing school and the hospital where I worked. He wrote about the interesting people he met.

One day I got a letter that stunned me. It was a proposal. He had it all planned: a ring, bought by a fellow student in East Berlin, was already on the way to me, and a letter to his best friend, asking him to do the honors on a special day, at a special time when we could be together in spirit. Of course, Hendrik added as an afterthought, it all depended if I would accept his proposal.

How could I respond to this quirky man who hated ceremony or celebration of any kind and tried to avoid them at all costs? He conveniently picked a safe distance, and asked a proxy to do the job. Where was the romance in all this?

I had one important question to ask: if it ever came to a wedding would he attend the ceremony or send a proxy?

"Of course I'll be there," he replied, "I love you."

So there I was, sitting on a chair with Hendrik's best friend Maurice—a handsome cavalier in a Frans Hals painting—on bended knee in front of me. He spoke the words of proposal Hendrik had written, put the plain gold band on my right hand, got up and kissed me on the cheek. It was a solemn moment. We drank a cup of coffee, and he left.

Hendrik died in 2007. Among his papers I found the note I had written on that day, 51 years before. It brought back wonderful memories of our beginning love. It read: proposal accepted, see you in church.

The Irony of Apartheid

Hendrik and I were married in February 1959. Before that, Hendrik had tried unsuccessfully to get his PhD in New Testament at the University of Pretoria. His dissertation proposal was summarily rejected by the faculty—all members of the ultra-conservative Dutch Reformed Church—as "too radical!"

He was not deterred by this setback. Instead he applied for a grant to the Alexander von Humboldt Foundation sponsored by the German Government, and was accepted. The stipend would cover his studies at the University of Bonn, and living expenses.

There were 180 recipients from all over the world who had received a grant. They came from countries like Japan, South America, Poland, Greece, Australia, and, to our surprise, three from South Africa, the land of Apartheid.

The president of West Germany, Heinrich Luebke, welcomed the recipients at an opulent reception in Villa Hammerschmidt, the official residence of the president. After that there were several trips arranged for sightseeing. One of them was a boat trip down the Rhine River.

The four hour boat trip from Bonn to Koblenz and back introduced us to some of the most spectacular and romantic sights in Germany. The mountains were dotted with ruins of medieval castles, and further down, centuries old, terraced vineyards cascaded down to the banks of the river. The grapes had just been harvested, and here and there yellow, rust colored leaves announced the arrival of fall.

But there was also a reminder of more recent history: the remains of the Ludendorff Bridge at Remagen, not far from Bonn. It was the last standing bridge over the Rhine during WWII, captured by the U.S 9th Armored Division, March 1945.

Travelling Beyond Borders

It was also an opportunity for the five of us South Africans to get acquainted. Hendrik and I told our brief history, and that Hendrik had plans to get his PhD in Theology at the University of Bonn. We knew by then that the other two men had a far more interesting background.

Daniel Verwoerd was the eldest son of Prime Minister Hendrik Verwoerd, elected in 1958. It was Verwoerd who, as minister of Native Affairs from 1950 to 1958, became known to the outside world as the "Architect of Apartheid."

Across from Daniel sat Neville Alexander, a victim of Verwoerd's relentless enforcement of Apartheid. Neville was from the Cape, and his bronze colored skin placed him in the category of Coloured people. What made him so was his maternal grandmother, who was an Ethiopian slave. That was all it took to put him there. Like his fellow Coloured people, he had no voting rights, and was restricted to living in areas designated for Coloured people only. He had a lively manner, displayed a sense of humor, and was fluent in German. His study grant would enable him to get his PhD in German Literature at the University of Tubingen. The rest of us were still trying to find our way through the grammatical obstacles of the German language.

During our conversation Neville—whose mother tongue, like ours, was Afrikaans—slyly remarked on the irony of meeting in a foreign country since such would not be possible in South Africa. As a Coloured man he would not be allowed to set foot on a boat with white passengers, let alone sit at the same table with the prime minister's son.

Daniel, mild mannered and soft spoken, did not take the bait. Smiling, he said, "I leave politics to my father."

His wife's reaction, however, was frostier. She defended the fairness of Apartheid policies as if she were addressing a person of low level understanding. Everyone, she said haughtily, was allowed to develop culturally in his own Bantu homeland and would eventually be allowed to vote for his own government. Naturally, she explained at the end of her lecture, that time was still a long way off and until then the whites had to take care of things for the benefit of ALL South Africans.

Neville only smiled and said no more.

At the end of our journey, back in Bonn, there were friendly goodbyes all round with vague, and empty promises to meet again whenever we were back in South Africa. That never happened.

Memory fails me: I don't remember what or where Daniel Verwoerd did his PhD or what eventually became of him.

With Neville it was different; we liked him very much and made plans to stay in touch even in Germany. There were a few visits, but time, studies, and the birth of our daughter Greta, took us on separate paths, and we lost track of Neville.

Years later, in 1964, when we were already living in the U.S., we got word that Neville had been arrested for so-called "subversive political activities." He had been sentenced to ten years on Robben Island, where he shared prison space with the most famous political prisoner, Nelson Mandela, until his release in 1974.

Hendrik and I could only surmise why Neville got arrested for subversive political activities. After the years in Germany where he was free to travel wherever he wanted, socialize with people of all races, eat at any restaurant he wanted, getting back to South Africa with a PhD in his pocket, to be forced back into the restrictions of Apartheid, must have been devastating.

Further notes on Neville Alexander:

After being released he did pioneering work in the field of language policy and planning in South Africa since the early 1980s. He was influential in respect of language policy development with various government departments, such as the National Language Project.

Neville was the recipient of the Linguapax Prize in 2008. The prize is awarded annually since 2000 in recognition of contributions to linguistic diversity and multilingual education. He had devoted more than twenty years of his professional life to defend and preserve multilingualism in the post-apartheid South Africa and became one of the major advocates of linguistic diversity.

Neville Alexander died August 27th, 2012, in Cape Town, South Africa.

Hendrik Verwoerd was stabbed to death in parliament by a white man on September 6th, 1966.

Welcome to America

The Ebola crisis that crossed over to America reminded me of our own experience when we first arrived in the United States.

It was an early Friday afternoon of the Labor Day weekend in 1962 when we arrived in New York. My husband, Hendrik, had earlier in the year been offered a teaching job at Emory's Candler School of Theology in Atlanta.

When we handed our passports to the official at the arrivals desk, he looked first at my husband and me, then at our just-turned-two daughter, Greta. He motioned for us to stand in an empty area just behind him, picked up the phone, and spoke rapidly to someone. A few minutes later a senior official arrived followed by a burly military policeman armed with a gun. We were surprised and stunned when he told us that our daughter could have smallpox; that we would be taken to a military hospital on Staten Island, put under quarantine for evaluation before we were allowed into the country.

I explained that the red spots on our daughter's face and arms were mosquito bites that she got when we spent the night in Amsterdam, and that Greta's obvious lethargy was because of almost two days of air travel. The official was not persuaded. He politely explained the reason for detaining us.

The day before our arrival a nine-year-old girl from India traveled with her family from New Delhi to Brussels and from Brussels to New York. They were allowed to fly on to Montreal, unaware that the child was infected with smallpox, a highly infectious viral disease. It was only at the Montreal airport that officials noted the symptoms of red pustules all over the little girl's body. They promptly called New York airport and ordered them to get in touch with all the passengers who were on the same plane from Brussels all the way back to New Delhi and warn them of possible smallpox infection. (At that time there were still no

Travelling Beyond Borders

computers that facilitated the tracking of passengers. It's hard to imagine how they coped with all the paperwork to avoid a potential smallpox crisis in the making.)

After hearing the official's explanation, I didn't bother to tell him our side of the story. We left Johannesburg late Wednesday afternoon, and arrived in Rome early the next morning. We had about six hours at our disposal to take a quick tour of the city. Part of it was in a horse drawn carriage that we thought would amuse Greta. But our little daughter was anything but enthusiastic. She sat between us listless and quiet. No wonder: we left a wintry cold South Africa, and landed in the heat of an August summer in Rome. We were all affected by the sudden climate change. After our tour we flew on to Amsterdam where we were to spend the night with my uncle and aunt.

My uncle, Dr. Jan de Jong, was the head pharmacist at the hospital of the University of Amsterdam located in the center of the city; that part where many of the houses dated back to the 17th century. The house they lived in since before the Second World War was next door to the hospital. The pharmacy was in the basement of their house, and they lived on the first and second floor.

Our bedroom with one large window looked out on a small courtyard behind the hospital where the garbage cans were kept, and what with the heat and small puddles of standing rainwater, it was the ideal condition to generate swarms of mosquitoes. Our window had no screen but we left it open anyway hoping for a cooling breeze in the hot and stuffy room.

It was only the next morning that we noticed that Greta, whose cot stood close to the window, was covered with red mosquito bites all over her face, neck, and arms. She was feverish, lethargic, and started vomiting soon after breakfast. My aunt took us to the hospital where a doctor examined her. He said her condition was a combination of mosquito infection, heat exhaustion, irregular sleep, and dehydration. I felt very guilty at that point and realized that small children don't travel well, especially under such trying circumstances.

The doctor gave us some soothing lotion for the itchy spots, and recommended that during our flight to New York we regularly give her sips of sugar water to give her energy, and keep her hydrated.

And so we arrived in New York early Friday afternoon only to be detained from flying on to Atlanta by over eager officials who tried to make up for their previous day's negligence!

There was no way out for us. The official did allow Hendrik to call the Associate Dean of Candler, Max Stokes, who was to pick us up at the Atlanta airport to tell him that we were detained in New York for the time being.

We followed the military policeman to a military car with glass partition between front and back seat, and drove on to Staten Island. He delivered us at a backdoor of the hospital, where we were received by a masked male person dressed from head to toe in protective garments. He unlocked a door close to the entrance, and showed us into a smallish room with two beds, a cot for Greta, and an adjacent bathroom. We were told not to leave the room under any circumstances, just ring the bell if we needed anything.

A while later another person also wearing protective gear came in to tell us that since it was Labor Day weekend we would have to wait till the following Tuesday for the specialist, who was off for the weekend, to check on Greta's rash. This was a blow!

Adding to our problems was that our luggage had been sent on to Atlanta. We had nothing! No change of clothes or sleepwear, other than hospital gowns. Hendrik refused to wear one.

I was furious about the whole situation and ready to take the first plane back to South Africa. What kind of welcome was this? And that in the shadow of the Statue of Liberty welcoming all visitors to the land of the, so called, free! I ranted on and on until Hendrik, ever the stoic, said that my anger would not change anything, and that we might as well make the best of it. The only good thing was that we had an air conditioner in the room that made our imprisonment bearable.

Travelling Beyond Borders

We were served food three times a day by masked persons, who slipped into the room, and walked out without so much as a greeting. Saturday went by without incident. On Sunday morning a friendly unmasked doctor wearing a white coat came into our room. He asked how we were, and what we were doing in the USA. Hendrik explained that we were from South Africa, and that he was appointed as assistant professor at Emory in Atlanta in time to begin teaching in September.

The doctor, who was not a specialist, examined Greta carefully, and confirmed that the red spots were indeed mosquito bites. He would sign release papers as soon as possible, and arrange for the military car to take us back to the airport after that. We thanked him for his help and kindness. It more than made up for the frustration and anger of the past few days.

We arrived in Atlanta later that afternoon, and picked up our luggage, took a taxi to the Emory campus where Max and his wife, Rose, welcomed us. They had reserved a large apartment for us in the Emory Student Center, with a cafeteria from where we could order food. A little unfurnished two bedroom house within walking distance of the campus, the dean told us, was being cleaned and newly painted before we could move in. With a beginning salary of only $6,500.00 per year, which gave us only enough to buy the bare necessities, the university generously provided a financial advance for us to buy the most necessary furniture to furnish the house.

The next day a young Emory doctor came to the apartment to examine Greta, free of charge, who was still not well. He said that food and liquids (meaning Coca-Cola), plus lots of sleep would cure her in no time, which is what happened. The apartment was quiet and allowed us all to relax and catch up on sleep.

Two weeks later we moved into our little house, and quickly settled down. Our neighbors were a mix of Emory colleagues, graduate students, and all of them were friendly and eager to help us feel at home. For us this finally turned out to be the real welcome to America!

A Radio Interview Brings Back Memories

Some five or six years ago I often listened to *Closer Look* on WABE hosted by Rose Scott from one pm to two pm.

What interested me were the people with remarkable stories that she talked to.

At some point she interviewed Derreck Kayongo, who was appointed to lead Atlanta's National Center for Civil and Human Rights. During the interview he told his story. He was born in Uganda during the dictatorship of Idi Amin who was known to the outside world as the butcher of Uganda for killing thousands of his people.

Derreck's parents, both teachers, lost their jobs, and fearing for their lives, fled Uganda to settle in Kenya where Derreck grew up. He made his way to the USA, and later became a citizen. He became known for his "save the soap" project among other things. Derreck created an organization all over the USA where cleaners of hotels and motels would, instead of throwing used and unused soap in the trash cans, collect them in a special container and take it to the manager's office. At some point a large container would be taken to some parts of Africa to be distributed to people where soap was scarce and used for washing themselves.

Rose Scott asked Derreck. "How did you come to settle in Atlanta?"

I was stunned when I heard his reply. "In the early seventies a black woman from South Africa, Tandi Gcabashe, invited me to come to Atlanta, and I've been living here ever since."

There was more to Derreck's interesting life, but my story is about Tandi Gcabashe whose name revived many memories.

Travelling Beyond Borders

At the beginning of the academic year at Emory University in the early eighties, my husband, Hendrik taught New Testament, a class required for incoming first year students of the Master of Divinity, or M. Div, program. On the first day a student walked into the classroom and introduced himself. His name was George Brink from the Cape in South Africa. Under Apartheid laws all Coloured—mixed blood of white, black, and Malaysian slaves—like George, were registered as separate from blacks because they had European features, were mostly lighter skinned, and spoke Afrikaans. But like all blacks in South Africa, they had no voting rights.

George told Hendrik that he and his wife Helen were settled in a small apartment in West Atlanta, and hoped we would visit them soon. Several weeks into the semester George and Helen invited us to a small party to meet two important members of the underground ANC, African National Congress, movement, and some other South Africans, refugees from Apartheid South Africa.

On the day of the party, however, Helen called to warn us that some of the more militant members of the ANC had threatened to disrupt the party and "harm any whites,"—meaning us—who showed up.

"We're coming," was all Hendrik said.

Despite initial awkward moments, the party went better than we anticipated. When one militant—with a malicious grin on his face—taunted Hendrik with, "We're going to kill every whitey in South Africa when we take over," Hendrik, with some humor, calmly stood his ground. After that everyone relaxed and came to talk to us.

The two guests of honor, Tandi Gcabashe and her husband Thulane were Zulus, but our introduction to them was met with a look of misgiving, even suspicion, from Tandi.

Hendrik, with his warm smile, won her over when he took her hand and greeted her in fluent Zulu. It was the beginning of a solid friendship that lasted many years.

Tandi was the daughter of Albert Luthuli who was the first African to receive a Nobel Peace prize in 1961. Luthuli was one of the founders of the ANC; leader of the non-militant faction of the ANC; also a Zulu tribal chief; and an educated teacher and mentor to emerging young leaders like Nelson Mandela.

Because of his political activities against the Apartheid regime he was banned to a small town, Groutville in Natal Province, where Tandi and her siblings grew up.

All her life Tandi was guided by her father's quest of peaceful negotiation with the Apartheid regime. That's how she ended up in Atlanta, to work for the American Friends Service Committee—a Quaker organization—of which she became director in 1981 until 1993. She traveled all over the US, campaigning against Apartheid, and while in Atlanta, verbally attacked the Coca-Cola Company for doing business in South Africa while many other companies complied with trade sanctions.

Back from her travels, Tandi would invite us for dinner or a get together to talk. But gradually Tandi and Hendrik got into the habit of having lunch together at their favorite Indian restaurant, particularly because Hendrik had become like an older brother in whom she could confide.

Life for Tandi was stressful. She had the care of three teenage children while her husband disappeared for months at a time on secret (sabotage?) missions that we could only guess at. No one, not even Tandi, knew where he was. It was a safety precaution against South African Government spies who kept a close eye on any members of the ANC living overseas, which explained the initial hostility of some people at the Brink's party.

In late 1989 Tandi called to tell us some important news. She was on her way to South Africa to visit her ailing mother and, to our stunned surprise, that her husband had filed for divorce. She had a notion that this would eventually happen and was okay with it. But there was something we could do for her: to keep her late father's personal papers that were of significant historical value. We were the only people she trusted, she said, to keep them safe. We ended up keeping them locked up in a fireproof filing cabinet in Hendrik's study for five years.

Albert Luthuli's papers were indeed valuable: among them a handwritten speech to a judge in court in 1960 after he was arrested for publicly destroying his passbook that all blacks had to carry at all times restricting them to certain areas.

"I stand before you Your Worship, charged with the destruction of my REFERENCE BOOK, and because of that with the crime of inciting my people to do the same "

There were letters written in the trembling hand of an old man; musings of a tribal chief; his life as a teacher; a lay preacher; as president of the ANC; and as a leading political activist against Apartheid. A life on paper.

All the while Luthuli was restricted to a fifteen mile radius in Groutville in Natal Province. Five years at a time. And every time a new reason was found to re-arrest him and deny him freedom of movement. In 1952 the minister of Native Affairs, Hendrik Verwoerd, who later became prime minister, offered Luthuli his freedom if he would give up his presidency of the Natal ANC movement and the chieftainship of his tribe. Luthuli refused. And was banned again.

When he won the Nobel Peace Prize in 1961—which one Afrikaans paper, *Die Transvaler* described as "an inexplicable pathological phenomenon"—the government reluctantly let him and his wife go to Oslo, for ten days, but banned him again when he returned.

In 1962 students of the University of Glasgow in Scotland elected him as Rector, to serve till 1965. But the government refused to let him go. Instead, the Student Representative Council created a Luthuli Scholarship Fund allowing a black South African student to study at the University of Glasgow for a year. Luthuli died of injuries in 1967 after being struck by a freight train near Groutville.

On July 22, 1967, newspapers reported:

"*Chief Albert Luthuli, Africa's first Nobel Peace Prize winner (1961) and president of the ANC (until his death), dies under mysterious circumstances on 21 July 1967, when he is struck by a train on a narrow railway bridge near his home in Groutville, near Stanger, Natal. Many of his followers believed more sinister forces were at work."*

Unlike Luthuli, Nelson Mandela evolved as the leader of the militant faction of the ANC, bent on overthrowing the South African government by any means possible.

In 1964 Nelson Mandela was arrested and sentenced to 27 years imprisonment to be served on Robben Island. For the Apartheid regime it was the ideal place to send all the militant political activists of the ANC movement.

The government described it as a "model prison," whatever that meant. The living conditions for prisoners were harsh: sitting in rows on a hard cement floor from sunrise till sunset in the hot sun breaking stones into gravel, one dirty blanket in their cells in cold winter months, forcing them to sleep in their clothes, and many other indignities.

When news reached the island in 1967 that Luthuli had died, the authorities gave Mandela permission to send a letter of condolence to his widow.

After serving seventeen years on Robben Island, Mandela was transported to a mainland prison, where he was treated for tuberculosis, and remained till his release in 1990.

In 1993 Tandi went to South Africa to help with the forthcoming election. The most important mission for her was to walk to the voting booth with her frail elderly mother, and help her cast a vote for the first time in her life. And to sit with her on the podium, an honored guest, for Mandela's inauguration as president of South Africa.

Several months later Tandi called us; she was not coming back to Atlanta for a while. President Mandela had asked her to be South Africa's ambassador to Venezuela. Then the question: what about her father's papers? They belonged to all the people of South Africa now. Hendrik said simply, "We'll bring them." And so in 1994 we boarded a plane and took Albert Luthuli's papers home.

We rented a small apartment for two weeks in a two story complex in the suburb of Arcadia, Pretoria. The building was directly across the street from the retirement home where my mother lived, and where we could visit her. At the back of the retirement home was a major street that separated the large piece of land where the government buildings, known as the Union Buildings, was situated.

A few days after our arrival, Tandi came to our apartment to pick up her father's papers that she would eventually hand over to the government archives. She was driven there by a chauffeur who parked at the entrance of the building while she visited us. Her reason was that she still did not feel safe in a white neighborhood: a clear indication that the stigma of apartheid was still in the mind of many blacks.

She was cheerful and giggling like a schoolgirl when she said, "Oh Eta (as she always called me) I have to go back to school." She explained that it was a diplomat school where all newly appointed diplomats could learn the details and nuances of good diplomacy. She left us soon after and we never suspected that this would be our last visit, and that we would never see her again.

NOTE:
A historical note of what a small world we sometimes live in needs to be added to this story. What Tandi didn't know, and Hendrik never told her, was that the suburb of Arcadia, including the hillside where the Union Building and the beautiful, terraced gardens slope down towards the street, was originally a farm established in 1857 by Hendrik's maternal great-grandfather, Andries Francois Du Toit, who named it "Arcadia." He was also responsible for the street layout, and Pretoria's first magistrate. The original map of the street layout is in the same archives where Luthuli's papers are stored.

Section VI: Travelling Companions

Appenzeller Cheese

Travelling Together

A Sabbatical Year in France

Dinner with a Priest

The Charming French

A Collection of Wine Labels

Appenzeller Cheese

"Can we meet in Zurich, rather than Amsterdam?" my mother asked over the phone.

Taken by surprise I blurted, "Why?"

Our original plan was that I fly from Atlanta, and she from Johannesburg, meet in Amsterdam then go on to the Northern Province of Groningen, where she was born: our final destination.

Since my father's death three years before—1978—my mother made an annual trip to visit with her extended family. She was fourteen years old in 1928 when her parents decided to settle on a farm in South Africa, and had never emotionally adjusted to living there. Holland was always her mother country.

She had invited me to go with her on this latest trip and I jumped at the opportunity. Two weeks free from taking care of husband, children, cooking and cleaning was just what I needed.

We met at the Zurich airport—she had arrived the day before—and took the train to the city. Our hotel was within walking distance from the station. Many foreign visitors, mostly businessmen, found it convenient to stay there.

As she always did, my mother showed me her wardrobe, specially made for this trip. For her a new wardrobe every time she went overseas, was half the fun of travelling. She also bought a new camera.

"I'm going to take many photos and send them to you afterwards."

I showed her my few mix and match outfits and the opera glasses my husband gave me as a gift.

"Are we going to the opera?" she asked with some consternation.

"No, no, I got them to take a closer look at some Chagall windows in the Frau Munster (Our Lady Church). It's not very far from here, we can walk there."

Opera was not my mother's cup of tea, but the Chagall windows (installed 1969–70) sounded intriguing. And that's how we spent the afternoon: taking turns to look at the beautiful stained glass windows behind the choir. It was a splendid melding of a 13th century church and 20th century modern art.

My mother had arranged for us to go on a bus tour the next day to the Canton (county) of Appenzell about two hours from Zurich. There we could take a cable car to the top of one of the highest mountains in the area, said to have a wonderful view of the region.

After an early supper we went to bed. In the middle of the night I was awakened by the sound of my mother gasping and whispering, "Oh my goodness! Oh my goodness!"

I looked at her bed and saw it was empty. Alarmed, I called, "Mamma?"

I heard a nervous giggle from the window. There she was, her tall silhouette outlined by the dim streetlight below, watching something through the opera glasses.

"Come see this," she said.

Across from the hotel I saw about five scantily clad women walking the pavement. The dark figures of a few men—hotel guests?—were talking to them; a couple paired off and disappeared into the side street.

"Well!" I said, "Who would have thought that the opera glasses could be used for this kind of entertainment too."

She couldn't sleep, my mother explained, probably from some jetlag, and looking out the window had been both shocked and fascinated to see prostitutes operating on the street below.

"I've never seen anything like this before. But enough of that now." she said. We got back into our beds. I heard her mumble, "Imagine having to earn a living like that," before I dozed off.

Travelling on the tour bus through the Swiss countryside brought back fond memories for my mother of all the travels she and my father had taken in the past. Beginning in 1948—on their first visit after the end of WWII—they fell in love with Switzerland and had since visited a different region every time they went to Europe. She wanted to see Switzerland again. "But I didn't want to do it alone, that's why I wanted us to meet in Zurich." I assured her that I was delighted to be her companion.

There were about twenty tourists on the bus all eager to get on the cable car to the top of the mountain. We were watching the first ten go up when my mother suddenly said, "I don't want to go up there, I'll wait for you on the bus. Here's my camera, you can take some photos."

I asked what the problem was, but she just kept saying she wasn't that interested in going up the mountain. I told the tour guide, a sympathetic young woman, and fluent in English, that my mother wanted to stay on the bus. She asked my mother if she had had a bad experience before. Clever woman: she had sensed my mother's problem.

My mother explained: when she and my father toured the Alps region in Italy in 1948, they went up with a cable car to get a view of the countryside. Halfway down the shaky cable car suddenly stopped with a jolt. There they were, hanging in midair; ten passengers cooped up in a claustrophobic stuffy little cabin; and a possible free fall of a thousand feet to the valley floor below.

Reliving that scary incident my mother blushed with embarrassment when she recalled how she became almost hysterical with fear, and that my father had to hold her close for over an hour, with her head resting on his shoulder, before the car started moving again. They got back on the ground without any further incident, but my mother decided then and there, "Never again!"

The tour guide said she could sympathize but this cable car was Swiss made and very solid. "Never had an accident." She gently coaxed my mother to go; she would go along with her and put her in a special seat, "and with your daughter next to you, you will be quite safe."

On the way up, my mother sat with her head bent down close to her lap, eyes closed, both hands holding on tightly to the seat until the cable car came to a stop.

It was a smooth ten minutes ride and the view from the terrace was spectacular. But just for a minute. As if on cue, a huge cloud came from nowhere, draped itself over the top of the mountain and stayed there. We couldn't see anything!

What to do? There were a few shops selling typical tourist kitsch, and a small restaurant that overlooked the terrace. We had about half an hour so we decided to have an afternoon snack-lunch. There wasn't much to choose from on the menu but the waitress recommended we try the Appenzeller cheese. It was a locally made raw milk cheese from cows that grazed on the clover rich pastures of Appenzell. "We serve it with crusty homemade bread, pickles and a light red wine. You can choose a glass or a small carafe." We chose a carafe, enough for one glass of wine for each.

The waitress brought the plates of cheese and two carafes of wine. "We ordered only one carafe," I told her. She apologized; she had misunderstood our order and reached to remove one carafe when my mother, who rarely drank wine, said, "Oh why not . . . we don't get to do this every day."

We had a lot to talk about, among others catching up on the usual family gossip. The half hour went by quickly and it was time to head back to the cable car. My mother needed to go to the "loo."

"The wine was a wee bit much," she said.

While she was putting on lipstick in the ladies' room my mother hummed a cheerful little tune and swayed her hips from side to side. All of a sudden, she started pulling funny faces in the mirror. We had a fit of laughter when I mimicked her and we competed to see who could pull the funniest face. I had never seen her act like this before, and then I realized my usually very dignified mother was tipsy! I asked how she felt.

"Oh I feel wonderful, light as a fairy," she said, waving her arms up and down to simulate flying.

Travelling Beyond Borders

By the time we boarded the cable car the cloud had lifted and the sky was beginning to clear but there was no time to take photos from the terrace. That didn't faze my mother; all the way down she cheerfully pointed her camera in all directions taking pictures of the countryside near and far.

On the way back to Zurich my mother thanked the tour guide for persuading her to go up the mountain; it had been a wonderful experience. We agreed that despite the cloud it had been a day well spent.

The next day we flew to Amsterdam where two of my mother's cousins met us and drove us to Groningen, two hours away.

A few weeks after I got back to Atlanta, I called my mother to ask how she was. "How did the photos you took from the cable car turn out?" I asked. She laughed, "They didn't. I forgot to take the lens cap off."

NOTE:

Marc Zakharovich Chagall was a Russian-French artist of Belarusian Jewish origin. An early modernist, he was associated with several major artistic styles and created works in virtually every artistic format, including painting, book illustrations, stained glass, stage sets, ceramic, tapestries, and fine art prints.

Travelling Together

Travelling through Europe always seems to bring out the worst and the best of our personalities in an otherwise uneventful marriage. There are shared euphoric moments, but more often than not we have long drawn out fights. We seldom fight at home. Hendrik, my husband, mild mannered and calm becomes unreasonable and prone to erratic behavior, and I, usually cheerful and loving, take on the role of long suffering wife and give him the silent treatment.

He sets the tone the moment we step into the rental car in Brussels.

"I am not setting foot in another castle or church this time," he announces firmly.

I love castles: history comes alive when you walk up narrow stone steps of a turret, or peer into a dungeon. Churches, in any shape or size appeal to me: walking down the aisle of a small 12th century church in a remote corner of Holland, where my two ancestors walked on November 15th, 1663, to get married, or sitting in the Cathedral of Strasbourg listening to a Bach cantata played by a master organist, or lighting a candle in Reims Cathedral in memory of someone. Those are the good moments we share.

But for my husband, once is enough. He wants to visit family and friends, spread out all over Europe. As always, I give in and say it's okay.

We are in Belgium on our way from Brussels to the medieval town of Louvain to have dinner with my cousin who wants to show us her new house. Hendrik drives, I have to read the road map. I hate reading the road map.

Close to Louvain, he wants to know where to turn next. I check the map and say, "at the next intersection, turn right."

He turns left. I shout, "I said turn right."

"No," he says, "the map must be wrong, I think it should be left," and drives on.

I put away the map and waited. After a while there are no more houses along the road, we are in rural country now. Asphalt stops and turns into dirt road. He drives on.

"Where are you going?" I yell.

"To Louvain," he says, eyes firmly focused on the road.

I give up, he's on his own. After a few miles the road ends abruptly at the gate of a cow pasture. The cows on the other side look up, stop chewing, stare at the car. This is my moment.

I sing loudly; "Welcome to Louvain!"

My victory is short lived. On the right road at last, he suddenly says, "Next time you should check the map more carefully and give directions that I can follow. You didn't seem to know which way to go."

I am stunned, speechless. What is it with men and their egos, I wonder. Why can't he just admit he's a stubborn idiot and have done with it? Instead, with adroitness that boggles my mind, he turns his stupid mistake into my fault. I'm furious. I say to myself, over and over, this is absolutely the last time I will travel with this man. Ever! I don't talk to him the rest of the way.

A few weeks later we are in France driving south through Provence. Our destiny is Orange, with the best preserved Roman Theater in Europe where, on a clear summer evening, visitors can hear Placido Domingo's soaring voice sing "Celeste Aida," and where pop music blares from a public system across the town square from eight in the morning till ten at night on market days.

But first we make a detour through the vineyards. This is Hendrik's country. He calms down, drives slower, looks around, and stops to take photos. We don't need a map; he knows the way.

"Let's get some wine," he suggests and I respond with an enthusiastic yes. We are soul mates here: we share the love of French food and exquisite wine.

At one vineyard cellar we choose two bottles of red wine priced way above our budget but we don't care, we decide to make up for it another time. Then it's on to Orange and our mansion turned hotel at the edge of town, far away from the loud pop music.

Two days later we have to get ready for the journey home. Everything is packed, the wine too. We will have our last dinner in the hotel restaurant. Hendrik looks quietly happy. I can't believe he is happy to go home. This is not like him.

"What's up?" I ask.

"Nothing," he says, smiling.

I don't pester him with my usual verbal tricks to tell me what's on his mind. I finish packing and get ready for dinner.

At the dining room door a woman tells us she is the chef's wife and will be our server. She takes us to a table in a more private corner of the dining room. I see candles on the table and the two bottles of wine we bought. Then he tells me: it's a surprise he planned for me. Earlier in the day he took the two bottles to the kitchen and asked the chef to create a gourmet dinner, just for us, to complement the wine. The chef was more than happy to comply.

When we are seated the chef comes to the table and tells us what we will have for dinner. It will be served the way we like it, French style: each dish served separately and in small portions. For the true gourmand it is the taste that counts. To begin, the chef serves a delicate fish dish, served with a white wine he chose and cooled to just the right temperature. Then dry French bread to clean the palate.

The chef's wife opens the first bottle of red wine, pours a little into each glass for us to taste. We agree, it is excellent, and fully complements the meat with wine sauce, and sautéed wild mushrooms on the side. There are small spoons beside the plate to spoon up the last of the sauce. A potato dish, baked to perfection, with just a hint of cheese, onion and herbs follows. After that we have a plain salad, no wine. More bread to clean the palate to prepare for dessert.

The chef rolls in a trolley with his own surprise for us. It's a creation of something that resembles a "bombe" only much lighter, covered with fresh strawberries over which he pours liquor and lights with typical French flair. He serves us a portion, still flaming, while his wife pours champagne into small glasses. My husband seldom eats dessert, but he cleans his plate to the last crumb.

Dessert is over, and now begins the true tasting of the wine, with an assortment of local cheeses.

"It is the cheese that makes the wine sing," says the chef.

How true. We spontaneously invite him and his wife to join us at the table and share the rest of the wine. They do, and he tells us how they came to live in Orange. He is Belgian, she is a born and bred Provencal and it was love of fine cooking that brought them together. The dinner lasts more than three hours.

Later my husband and I sit alone on the darkened porch of the hotel, sipping espresso. It is quiet and we breathe in the fragrance of lavender bushes in full bloom close by. I thank him for a perfect evening. We agree; it was a wonderful trip after all.

We will do it again next year.

A Sabbatical Year in France

My husband Hendrik had a trace of French blood in his veins that went back to his mother's ancestors, French Huguenots who, at some point, fled from Lille to settle in the Cape of Good Hope, South Africa.

So it was no surprise to me when he announced that he wanted to spend his sabbatical leave from Emory University, 1981–82, in France. The problem was where to go. Hendrik called his friend and colleague, Father Jean de Lorme and asked for advice.

"Come to Lyon!" Jean said. "I'll find you a place to stay."

A few weeks later he called with good news. He had found us a fully furnished apartment, linens included, and low rent . . . in a convent!

Hendrik was delighted.

"This is going to be an interesting adventure my love," he cheerfully told me.

I wasn't so sure. I couldn't imagine living in a convent for a year, we weren't even Catholic. What restraints would the nuns impose on us? What effect would this have on our fourteen-year-old twin daughters, Johanna, and Maria, who would have to go to a French school a few blocks from the convent? For our teenage twins, who knew very little French in the beginning, the transition from an American school to a French one bordered on trauma. But within a month they had become immersed in school life and the ways of their fellow students—who tried out their flimsy knowledge of English on them.

We arrived in Lyon in late August after an exhausting two day journey from Amsterdam airport—where we picked up our new Volvo—and on the way spent the night in a small town called Waterloo where the twins showed no interest in the history of the place but, in typical teenage fashion, swooned over their first taste of profiteroles in the hotel restaurant.

Travelling Beyond Borders

The large convent-hospital complex, home to the nuns of St Francis of Assisi, sat on top of a hill in the suburb of Croix Rousse. On either side of this elevated land the rivers Rhone and Saone embraced just south of it to become the Grand Rhone which tumbled its way through deep mountain gorges, meandered passed the swampy Camargue where wild white horses roamed and flamingos nested, and finally melded with the Mediterranean sea.

Our apartment was on the ground floor of a large 400-year-old house separated by a small parking lot for attending doctors across from the hospital, and a reserved parking space for our car. The *Aumonier*, who served mass to the nuns twice a day in the small chapel wedged between our house and the convent, lived upstairs. He turned out to be a master organist and many Saturday afternoons Hendrik and I quietly slipped into the back of the chapel and listened for a few hours.

"A concert just for us," we said.

The apartment was furnished with seemingly donated or discarded furniture just enough to make it livable, but all very clean and proper. The only luxury was an under the counter refrigerator. No dishwasher, washer or drier. We could exchange bed linens every two weeks before 10am, but our clothes had to be hand washed. Hendrik bought me a portable washing machine, a drying rack above the bathtub, and to everyone's delight, a small television.

It was oppressively hot that August in 1980, and with no air-conditioning and no screens in the windows, allowing hordes of flies to find their way to the kitchen by day and swarms of whining mosquitoes to torture us at night, I was ready to get back on the next plane headed for Atlanta.

But there were other things that made up for the lack of luxuries: the friendliness of the few nuns we met who were in charge of running the hospital and convent—in particular Soeur Bernadette Nourdin, a small plump motherly woman, who managed the business affairs of the convent. Most of them were nurses who took care of the patients in the hospital; the rest cooked and cleaned.

Hendrik became enamored with the nuns after they invited him and the Aumonier to their sitting room to talk and drink their home made beer. "That's my kind of nuns!" he told me with some glee after the visit. Besides the Aumonier he was the only male who had ever been invited into their sitting room and he couldn't wait to tell his friends in Atlanta how good life in a convent was.

Then there was the farmer's market on the Boulevard de la Croix Rousse a half block from the convent. The boulevard bisected the suburb of Croix Rousse into the Upper Level—the top of the hill where the convent stood—and the Lower Level which gradually terraced down to the city of Lyon.

We made another discovery: the market was famous all over France for the variety of foods you could buy—anything from exotic cheeses to a stall that sold only tripe. This was where famous chefs like Paul Bocuse, followed by a retinue of sous-chefs, decided the menu for his restaurant on the outskirts of Lyon.

It was not just the famous and wealthy who bought here. Locals and country folk found their way here too, even foreigners like us.

It is still early in the morning on market day. As I walk along the long rows of tables and portable glass counters I am overwhelmed by the choice of vegetables, fruits, meats and trays filled with a variety of olives and anything else that can be pickled, next to a glorious display of flowers. Almost at the end of the market I am surprised and delighted to see an Arab selling *outspan* oranges from South Africa—this in the time of trade sanctions against the Apartheid regime. I ask him where the oranges come from. "From Israel," he replies nonchalantly. I buy eight, and proudly carry them home, thinking about the irony of world politics.

On another day I pass a table where a butcher sells live chickens and dead rabbits. An old woman, black dress down to her ankles, grey hair tied in a grandma knot, pokes her walking stick into a cage of frantically squawking chickens, pointing out the chicken of her choice. The butcher seems to know her; he hands over the squawking chicken, legs tied with string, which she unceremoniously stuffs in a shopping bag and carries home for that night's supper. I'm not that brave. I prefer them dead, plucked, and headless.

A little way further another butcher sells beef, veal, and pork from a portable counter. I turn away in disgust when I see a few flies crawl over the meat, and a few others buzzing against the glass trying to get out. I decide to buy my meat at the next butchery.

The small impeccably clean butchery is run by a family of four: father, mother—who works the till—and their twin sons. The father and his sons are tall, handsome, and with their blond hair and moustaches, resemble Viking warriors of yore. But that's where the romance ends. One of the sons asks what I want. I point to a cleaned ready to cook chicken and when I look up as I place my order, a pair of crossed-eyes meets my gaze.

Imagine a cross-eyed butcher with a hefty meat cleaver in his hands! I look at his twin and see he is cross-eyed too. I can't decide if they are playing the fool with me, a foreigner, or really cross-eyed. I go to the mother, a mousy looking woman, and when I hand her the money, I see she is cross-eyed too. I glance at the father, just to make sure, but his clear blue eyes look straight into mine, an amused smile on his lips.

It's late October. The air is crisp and invigorating, and I'm at the market trying to decide what to cook for dinner. Hendrik no longer walks with me to help with my meager knowledge of French. Some of the sales folks recognize me and smile encouragingly as I point to what I want.

Then I see a stall that sells Poulet de Bresse—a chicken from a region about sixty kilometers north of Lyon. The chickens, specially fed, are famous for their exquisitely tasty meat and priced way above ordinary chickens. I buy one, plucked, headless but with the innards still intact. I have visions of a beautiful roasted chicken on a large platter, surrounded by exotic vegetables and served with a side dish of Gratin pommes de terre a la Lyonnaise.

At home I soon realize that there is a difference between the human anatomy and that of a chicken. I don't know where the gall bladder is. Julia Child's' voice on TV, "Be careful not to break the gallbladder, it will spoil the taste of the meat," rings in my ear. I cut the bottom hole a bit bigger and try to look inside. It's dark in there. I end up cutting the chicken into small pieces. No stuffed roast chicken tonight. It will be pan fried, the stuffing becomes creamy mushroom sauce, and the Gratin Lyonnaise becomes plain mashed potatoes.

At table I eagerly ask my family what they think.

"Tastes like chicken." Hendrik says.

The twins agree. "It's okay Mom, the mashed potatoes are wonderful."

I'm suddenly glad I didn't tell them the chicken cost $20.00. From now on it will be simple farm chicken with the innards removed.

Jean de Lorme came to visit soon after we were settled. The twins were happily adjusting to their new school, named after native son, author, WWII pilot, Antoine de Saint Exupéry, and Hendrik was getting ready to work on his studies.

"Have you discovered the Beaujolais river yet?" Jean asked.

We looked puzzled. "Is it on the map?" Hendrik asked.

"No, no," Jean laughed. "It's not really a river. That's what the locals call the 'river of wine' that flows from the Beaujolais vineyards through Lyon to the rest of Europe and beyond, right to the shore of your country. Go for a visit as soon as you can."

It was harvest time and glorious weather in mid-September when we cruised through the vineyards. Names like Julianas, Moulin a Vent, Chenas and Fleurie, all red wines, tempted us to stop at each vineyard where you could taste before you bought.

I fell in love with Fleurie. "A woman's wine," Hendrik teased.

"No wonder," I replied, "It's charming, elegant, flowery, fruity and not cheap." We bought two bottles to start our collection.

We tried Moulin a Vent and Julianas next. Hendrik liked Moulin a Vent; I liked

Julianas, but we didn't argue, as we sometimes did, about who has better taste; we bought two bottles of each.

Through the sabbatical year friends and family found their way to the convent: cousins from Holland; friends from Germany; my mother flew in from South Africa; and our friend Louis Lane from Atlanta and his friend Herbert, stopped by for a few days, before he went on to Johannesburg where he was to be the guest conductor of the Johannesburg Philharmonic Orchestra during the summer.

Months before his visit Louis reserved a table at *La Pyramide* in Vienne, about twenty kilometers south of Lyon. Between the two world wars, it was THE restaurant in all of France and the chef/owner Fernand Point the mentor/teacher for other famous chefs like Paul Bocuse. Famous people like Winston Churchill, actors, authors, and other important people dined there. The Duchess of Windsor, Wallis Simpson, so the story goes, found refuge from harassing paparazzi in the home of the Point family before her marriage to the besotted Duke.

Vienne, like Lyon dates back to Roman times. Before dinner we looked at a Roman temple on the market square and a small Roman pyramid—from which the restaurant got its name.

The restaurant was in a large mansion surrounded by a garden on a quiet street. It only catered to about fifty people and we were the lucky ones to get a table at such short notice. Fernand Point was no longer living, but his widow, Madame Point wandered from table to table to ask if the diners were happy. We were.

I got my first taste of escargot. It was delicious. (The French language is ideally suited to make disgusting things like slimy snails sound elegant.) I chose lamb for the main dish; the three men chose beef. Louis ordered an expensive red wine for us. The sommelier gently advised him to choose a cheaper but very appropriate wine that would go well with our food. No where but in France! It's the taste that's important not how much money you spend.

This dinner was the highlight of our stay in Lyon. But we also frequented small restaurants—hidden from tourists in narrow side streets—where the locals ate cassoulet and quiche, and ending, as always, with baguette and a variety of cheeses accompanied with cheap wine.

Our stay in the convent was coming to a close. Soeur Bernadette Nourdin invited us to visit the small farm the convent owned in the countryside, far away from the vineyards. That's where a staff of younger nuns took care of the old retired and sick nuns who, after a life of selfless service, found their final resting place under sheltering trees in the cemetery.

It was peaceful and quiet on the farm. Two nuns took us on a tour of the home, the large vegetable garden, and the orchard, that supplied the convent, and also where their beer was made. In a nearby enclosure free range chickens provided meat and eggs.

We drank homemade, honey sweetened chamomile tea on the terrace with a glorious view that stretched far into the distance. "We can watch the sunset from here," one of the nuns told us. When we left, they presented us with a dozen fresh eggs and a jar of preserved figs. "You eat it with a spoon," one nun advised. We drove back to Lyon impressed with how at peace they were with life in a convent.

It was time to pack up and say goodbye to many friends and acquaintances we had met during the year. The twins were reluctant to leave Lyon and their newfound friends in school who promised to stay in touch. Hendrik was reluctant too, but students and teaching were awaiting his return to Emory. I was the least sad. It was a good year, but with the hot July summer fast approaching I looked forward to my air conditioned house, and the luxury of a dishwasher and a dryer. Besides, I had gained twenty pounds and needed a new wardrobe.

NOTE:

Antoine Marie Jean-Baptiste Roger, Comte de Saint-Exupéry, simply known as Antoine de Saint-Exupéry, was a French writer, who became famous for his story *The Little Prince*, a poet, an aristocrat, a journalist, and pioneering aviator. He became a laureate of several of France's highest literary awards and also won the United States National Book Award.

Born: June 29, 1900, Lyon, France
Died: July 31, 1944, when his plane disappeared into the Mediterranean Sea.

Other books by Saint Exupéry:

Airman's Odyssey
Flight to Arras
Night Flight
Southern Mail
Wartime Writings
Wind, Sand and Stars

Dinner with a Priest

"As soon as you're settled," Jean De Lorme said over the phone, "You must all come to Annecy for the day."

"Settled," meaning that my husband, Hendrik, and I, and our fourteen-year-old twins, were at the beginning of a sabbatical year (1981–82) in France. Not only that but adjusting to living in a convent run by the nuns of St. Francis of Assisi. It was Jean who had found us this unusual and somewhat intriguing place to stay.

The convent complex was surrounded by a high iron fence and a gate that was locked promptly at 10pm, every day. We got our own key.

When we were settled, we were ready to visit Jean in Annecy and see the region that he fondly called "my country" in the Haute Savoie.

Our host, a Catholic Priest-professor who commuted to Lyon every two weeks to teach New Testament at CADIR, Centre pour l'Analyse du Discours Religieux, welcomed us to his house with open arms.

"Come, I want to show you my country," he said soon after we had had something to drink. Not the medieval town, as I had hoped, but a drive into the surrounding mountains. He wanted to go to the top of the mountain, he said, to show us the view.

As he drove up ever higher on precarious cow paths, my heart nearly stopped a few times. All I could think of was crashing down to the valley floor. But Jean was a secure and safe driver and we finally reached the top. The view of the French Alps and snow covered Mont Blanc in the distance was indeed breathtaking. And from the valley far below we heard the musical clanging of cow bells where cows grazed in sweet pastures.

"*Je'aime mon Pays,*" Jean said quietly. (I love my country.)

We all understood then why this peaceful spot was more important to him than a stuffy medieval town.

After we had inhaled our quota of fresh air, Jean took us home for dinner. Cecile, Jean's housekeeper, who spoke with the typical sing-song accent of her native Haute Savoie, invited us into the dining room.

The setting was simple: a long dining table covered with an oil cloth surrounded by unmatched chairs standing on an uneven floor of a 400-year-old house. Many guests had gladly gathered there before and we soon found out why.

Cecile brought a large bowl filled with stew to the table. "Ragout du Lapin," she explained to the twins who looked with some suspicion at the offered bowl.

"Rabbit stew," Jean translated.

"We're eating a baby rabbit?" one twin wailed, sounding like a petulant five-year-old. "No thanks."

Embarrassed by such a display of bad manners I glared my displeasure. Jean just laughed.

"No, no," he explained, "This was an old rabbit." He encouraged them to take a few bites. They politely did so, but I could tell from their faces that they would never eat rabbit stew again. That was the only hiccup of the meal, though.

As we soon discovered, to our delight, every dish was served separately. Meat was followed by walnut sized potatoes soaked in homemade butter, tender green beans, and cauliflower in a delicate cheese sauce. All accompanied with thick slices of baguette to clean up traces of the previous dish. Then a green salad. And rich flavorful wine throughout. The conversation flowed and there was much laughter.

Most of this bountiful repast came from Jean's garden, a small plot of carefully tended land on the outskirts of Annecy. For dessert we had tiny fresh peaches, peeled, and pitted, floating in a rhubarb sauce.

Our meal done, Jean suggested to the twins that they take a walk in the area close to his house. There would be much to see: the medieval water canal flowing passed his house, the wide bridge over it where regional farmers sold their wares, cozy shops luring tourists inside and sidewalk cafes surrounded by tubs of brightly colored flowers. They jumped at the opportunity, not only to look at the scenery, but, as they confessed later, to check out the local boys sauntering about.

Meanwhile we adults sat around the dining table drinking herb tea gathered from Cecile's herb garden. When our cups were empty, Jean poured a small portion of homemade liqueur into them—no fancy glasses here.

We drove back to Lyon in the late afternoon, filled by the wonder of the day. We had been introduced to the *real* France by a charming priest and his dedicated housekeeper. A simple way of life: no need for damask, crystal glass or polished silver to enhance the spontaneous warmth of developing friendship, and laughter at our humorous attempts to bridge the language barrier. Even the twins ended the day with an enthusiastic, "Let's go back there again . . . soon."

The Charming French

In September 1989 my husband, Hendrik and I went on our usual annual trip to Europe. It was mainly to visit friends and family, but this time we decided to make a pilgrimage to Lyon in the south of France. We had spent a wonderful sabbatical year there in 1981/82: living in a hospital-convent complex run by the nuns of St. Francis of Assisi.

This trip, Hendrik and I were alone. On our last afternoon in Lyon we decided to walk to my favorite shopping mall, Part Dieu, in downtown Lyon and then go to Hendrik's favorite restaurant, Brasserie Guillaume Tell.

Close to the shopping center, I tripped in a small pothole and fell on my face, smashing my sunglasses into and around my left eye and also injuring my left knee and foot. We managed to get to the restrooms, where I wanted to attend to my wounds and clean up as best I could.

The elderly woman attendant in the ladies' room took one look at me and said, "Ah Madame, you are injured."

Before I could say anything, she took my hand and walked me to the first aid station close by where she instructed the medical assistant to take care of me. He cleaned my wounds ever so gently and assured me that my eye was not permanently damaged. All this for free.

When I walked out, I saw Hendrik and, to my surprise, the woman attendant who had waited at the door all the time to make sure I was okay. I did not look very pretty: there was a cut and bruise on my forehead, my left eye was blue and swollen and I limped on a painful foot.

In spite of my injuries, I insisted we go to the restaurant anyway. Once there Hendrik, who was a firm believer of Johnny Walker Scotch as a cure for whatever ails you, suggested we sit in the little garden of the restaurant and have a Scotch before going in for dinner. I had never had Scotch before and was surprised how much better I felt after the first few sips.

When the head waiter took us to our table, he looked at me closely and asked if Hendrik had beaten me. I nodded yes. When our waiter came to the table the headwaiter pointed to Hendrik with mock amazement and said, "Look what he did! He looks so innocent!"

We all laughed and then I explained what had really happened.

Since I spoke French only in the present tense, I said "I am falling."

Tactfully hiding his amusement, the headwaiter gave Hendrik a short lecture on how to treat a lady when you take her out to dinner. By way of example he came to our table again after dinner, took my arm in his and escorted me to the door, while Hendrik followed us with a sheepish smile.

Fortunately the bus that would take us back to the hotel stopped in front of the restaurant. On the way Hendrik asked the driver if he could stop in front of the hotel so that I didn't have to walk too far. "Of course!" he replied.

At the hotel entrance he motioned to Hendrik to be careful while he helped me down the steps of the bus, and when I was safely on the curb, drove off waving and shouting a cheerful, "Good night and speedy recovery!"

A Collection of Wine Labels

I always knew that my husband, Hendrik, was a collector of rare things: tools, books, stamps and currency from countries all over the world. Still, it was a surprise to find a collection of wine and liquor labels in a box among the vast collection of sound recordings of classical music he kept in the basement. Many of these labels brought back memories of where we were and what we did. Here are a few.

Slivovitz. Plum brandy from Serbia.

We were on Sabbatical leave in Lyon, France in 1981 when our best German friends, Margret and Paul Gerhard Schoenborn, invited us to go on a once-in-a-lifetime trip to Berlin. Paul Gerhard wanted to revisit the city where he had attended a pastor's conference in East Berlin in 1961 and managed to escape to West Berlin just in time before the wall went up.

We were living in Bonn at that time. Hendrik was finishing his doctoral dissertation at the University of Bonn where Paul Gerhard had just graduated with a degree in theology, to become a pastor, while Margret graduated with a major in sociology and English. I was taking care of our one-year-old daughter Greta who was born in Bonn in 1960.

The plan was to travel by car to the medieval town of Helmstedt on the border between West and East Germany to get on the only Autobahn (Freeway) that visitors from West Germany were allowed to use to go to Berlin.

We seemed to be the only travelers on the road that day. Much of it was in desperate need of repair. No wonder.

"It was one of the many Autobahns built by Hitler in the thirties," Paul Gerhard told us, as a quick way to move his armies and military equipment towards

Berlin and beyond to attack Poland and other countries as part of his plan to incorporate them all into the "Great Third Reich." And after the war, repairing the autobahn that led to the West was not part of Russia's plan when it occupied East Germany. There were people to control and a devastated economy to build up.

All along the Autobahn I was struck by the isolation and ghostly stillness that pervaded the vast treeless landscape. No sign of life anywhere, no birds in the sky.

Even at the halfway stop where travelers could buy gas, snacks, and use the not very clean bathroom, run by an elderly couple, there was a stillness that made us talk in hushed voices. It was there that Hendrik spotted a few bottles of Slivovitz from Serbia on a shelf. He promptly bought one for us to try after Paul Gerhard explained that it was plum brandy, a favorite drink of East Europeans.

We arrived in West Berlin late in the afternoon and spent the night in the spacious apartment of friends of Margret and Paul Gerhard, whom they had known since their student days. She was a dentist he one of the official coordinators of cultural events. They told us about the best museums to visit during our two day visit.

The Pergamon museum in East Berlin was the one that interested us the most because it would also give us an opportunity to see what life was like in the Eastern zone of Germany after the devastation of WWII. The only way to get to East Berlin was through Checkpoint Charlie in the American sector. What a difference a few hundred yards made! On the West side it was all happy bustle, people walking along colorful shops, restaurants and streets filled with busy traffic passing by.

On the East side it was quiet with hardly any traffic; people wore dull expressions and drab grey clothes; even the food in the small café where we stopped for a light lunch was bland and tasteless. What passed for coffee was an undrinkable brown brew that we couldn't identify. And then the sauntering soldiers with guns

Travelling Beyond Borders

watching our every move, so it seemed, as we made our way to the Pergamon museum located on the Bodestrasse close to other museums.

I didn't know what to expect when we entered the museum, but I was stunned by the beautiful display of artifacts. We all were. Such a sharp contrast of the pervading gloom outside. But it wasn't always so. The museum was built in a time when East Berlin was still part of the vibrant metropolis of an undivided Germany.

One of the most interesting artifacts was the western side of the Pergamon altar, dating back to the first half of the 2nd century B.C. —hence the name of the museum which was specially built in 1930 to house it. The altar was partly destroyed by Allied bombing during the war but completely restored in the fifties. The Ishtar Gate—known as the Eighth Gate into the inner city of Babylon and built in 575 B.C. by king Nebuchadnezzar—was another impressive artifact that displayed the artful use of colorful tiles covering the two stories high walls. And though the city of Babylon is long gone the gate is a reminder of what a beautiful city it must have been. [The Pergamon altar and Ishtar Gate are still in the Pergamon Museum in Berlin. Check them out on Google. Very impressive!]

We left Berlin the next day travelling on the Autobahn back to West Germany. At the halfway stop Hendrik found another bottle of Slivovitz, this time from Bulgaria.

In what seemed like an almost bizarre twist of fate we happened to be on another sabbatical leave in Marburg, Germany in 1989 when the Berlin Wall came down.

Here's an excerpt from the Christmas letter I wrote to family and friends.

"As fate would have it, we were here 28 years ago when the first bricks for the wall were laid. We shared some anxious hours with our friend Margret Schoenborn whose then fiancé, Paul Gerhard, happened to be at a meeting in East Berlin. A phone call reassured her that he was already back in the West when the wall went up.

"Every East German visitor to West Germany receives DM 100.00 (Deutsch Mark) as *'begruesungsgelt'* ("Hello" money) because they can only bring DM.15.00 into the West, and that doesn't buy much. There was the young man who discovered a can of caviar that sold for DM.8,550.00. 'That's my salary for the year!' he exclaimed in amazement.

"As always there's a mix of good and evil, even when such historic events happen. Most East Germans are stunned at the variety of groceries especially fresh fruits and vegetables that are available. So some charlatan shopkeepers promptly tripled the prices to make a profit. (May they roast in the Here After!)

"On the other hand there were visitors who told of being invited by total strangers for dinner, or spend the night or who received bills of money from passersby. We share the euphoria of so many Germans but it has already become clear that once it settles, some hard economic facts will have to be worked out on both sides. In the meantime Bundeskanzler (president) Kohl has announced a ten point plan for the 're-unification' of Germany, an untimely and disturbing move for some Germans. (Higher taxes and so on.)"

Vin D'Alsace. Riesling, Tokay, Muscat

It was a trip Hendrik and I took to Alsace in 1989 where we met Margret and Paul Gerhard there to go wine tasting and check out the cultural landscape.

The four of us went to Turckheim, the best place to taste and buy Alsace wine. Margret was in her element. "What a wonderful way to take in minerals," she said as we tasted first, Riesling, then Tokay and Muscat, a dessert wine. We stocked up on all three wines. Hendrik, always a stickler for doing things right, bought a dozen of the traditional green stemmed glasses for Alsace wine to add variety to his collection of glasses.

Our next trip was to the village of Gunsbach to see the house where Albert

Schweitzer grew up. He became famous for the hospital he founded in Lambarene in West Africa in 1913 and where he died there on September 4th, 1965.

Hendrik and Paul Gerhard were particularly interested in Schweitzer who studied at the University of Strasbourg and ended up with four doctoral degrees: Theology, Philosophy, Music, specializing in Bach's organ music, and Medicine. Both of them owned and had read Schweitzer's book, *The Quest of the Historical Jesus*, a book that influenced Hendrik to write *Who was Jesus?* published in 1989, and dedicated to Paul Gerhard.

We followed up on a trip to Strasbourg where we went to a midday concert in Strasbourg Cathedral to hear a master organist play Bach, on the same organ where Schweitzer played before he went to Lambarene.

Schweitzer, who won the Nobel Peace Prize in 1952 for campaigning against nuclear development, grew up speaking the Alsatian dialect, akin to German, in a time when Alsace was still part of Germany. I had a special interest in languages since early childhood and hoped I could hear someone speak Alsatian. My wish was granted when the owner of the bed-and-breakfast where Margret and Paul Gerhard stayed, suggested we walk up to the other side of the hills behind her house where we would find an old, still working farm and where the farmer's wife served dinner for up to twelve visitors. We walked up the hill as the sun went down, passing overgrown trenches, now eerily quiet, that were dug during the first world war and where thousands of soldiers died.

We sat on benches with other visitors around a long wooden table in a large room lighted by petroleum lamps. There was no menu, you ate what the friendly farmer's wife—who spoke Alsatian—cooked and served that day. No wine, only locally brewed beer. It was a simple but delicious meal. At the end of the meal we were served Muenster cheese, a smelly but favorite local cheese made from cow's milk that went well with Alsace wine. Hendrik was so enamored that he promptly bought some the next day to take back to Marburg. Paul Gerhard wanted to buy one too, but Margret just said, "You're NOT bringing that stinky cheese into my house!" and that was that.

Amontillado. Medium dry sherry from Spain.

In 1987 a Danish movie, *Babette's Gaestebud* (*Babette's Feast*), hit the market and was awarded the prize as best international movie of the year. It was based on a story written by Isak Dinesen who became famous for her book *Out of Africa*.

An enthusiastic friend urged us to see the movie. Hendrik reluctantly agreed (that was not his thing, he said), but by the end of the movie he was hooked. Not only that, when we watched the video again later with Margret and Paul Gerhard, he bought a bottle of Amontillado because that was what Babette served with one of her dishes. While we watched Babette prepare her spectacular feast, we raised a few glasses in her honor. Babette also introduced us to Veuve Cliquot, a pricy French champagne that she served with a meat dish! An eye opener for us but which we only bought and enjoyed on special occasions.

Paul Gerhard was the only one who could follow the movie in Danish while the rest of us had to rely on English subtitles. His interest in Danish and the Danish people began many years ago when he became almost obsessed with researching the life and time of one of Denmark's most beloved playwrights, poet and Lutheran pastor, Kaj Munk (Moonk), who was murdered by the Gestapo during the German occupation of Denmark. His crime was to speak out against the Nazi occupation and in particular the treatment of Jews.

On a cold wintry day in January 1944, while he was preaching in the church of St. Sebastian in Vederso, of which he was pastor, Gestapo officers walked in, dragged him from the pulpit and arrested him. A simple cross marks the spot where his bullet ridden body was later found in a ditch beside a country road.

Kaj Munk was buried close to the main entrance of his beloved St Sebastian church. The simple tombstone only mentioned his date of birth and the date of his death in 1944. It is surrounded with plants and flowers.

Margret and Paul Gerhard were children during the war years. Just like children all over Europe, they experienced years of hunger and the trauma of seeking shelter in basements when bombs rained down from the sky and turned towns and cities to rubble.

But unlike other children they grew up in a country where the stigma of the "Evil German" would affect them for the rest of their lives. Paul Gerhard's father was a soldier, killed during battle in Russia and buried somewhere in an unmarked grave. Although his father was not a Nazi or even sympathetic to the cause, he was still a soldier fighting for Hitler, a thought that added to Paul Gerhard's burden of guilt.

Paul Gerhard realized he could not make up for his Germanness by tackling all the atrocities of the Nazi regime. Instead, he focused on one martyr, Kaj Munk. That prompted him to learn Danish in order to translate some of Munk's best known plays into German. It took him many years to bring this about, but finally two of the plays were performed on stage in Germany and became an instant hit.

A year after Hendrik's death in 2007, I received a letter from Paul Gerhard with the news that he and Margret went to Denmark to attend the Christmas Eve church service in Vederso where Kaj Munk had served as pastor for so many years. The two of them stood in front of the pulpit and Paul Gerhard once again told the story of Kaj Munk. Then the two of them began to sing "Silent Night, Holy Night" in German. Some of the Danish congregants, among them Kaj Munk's family—who through the years had become close friends—stood up and joined them at the pulpit. In the end the whole congregation joined in, many singing in German others in Danish. "Margret and I were moved to tears," he wrote. "It felt like acceptance and redemption, at last."

Hendrikus Wouterus Boers

Hendrik and Ida's Engagement

Blue China Cups

Hendrik and Ida's Wedding

Hendrik studying, University of Bonn

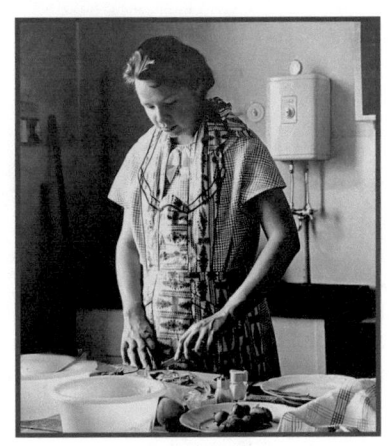

Ida cooking

Hendrik and Ida drinking tea

Ida waving at the window, Bad Godesberg, Germany

Hendrik meets President Heinrich Luebke

Highveld. Gauteng, South Africa

Croix-Rousse market, Lyon, France

Hendrik's conviviality

Cheese stall, Croix-Rousse market

Vineyards, Beaujolais, France

Hendrik's ten-foot workbench

Hendrik at his computer

Workshop shelves and marmalade jars

Hendrik and Ida holding hands

Remembering a husband

Section VII:
After Hendrik

Who is This?

Remembering a Husband

Who Is This?

My husband died in 2007. Some years after this, I finally decided to donate his books to the Pitts Theology Library at Emory University. It was a collection that began in Hendrik's student years in South Africa and grew close to three thousand books during his 35 year career as a professor at Emory.

My decision to donate this valuable collection did not go without some emotion and a touch of sadness. But the thought that most of the books would benefit students and faculty alike inspired me and I knew would have had Hendrik's decided approval.

I called my friend Pat Graham, the director of the library and told him that he was welcome to take as many of Hendrik's books as he wanted. He reacted with enthusiasm; he wanted them all. He knew that Hendrik had a collection that contained many out of print books that Pitts could use to replace "lost" books in the stacks or add to the library's already considerable holdings.

The long rows of now ghostly empty shelves in the basement were a stark reminder that along with the books, part of me and memories of the many authors who through the years became friends, colleagues or mentors to Hendrik, had gone out the door too, and brought an end to a phase in my life.

A few weeks later I received a surprising e-mail from Pat with the question: "Who is this?"

I opened it and saw a black and white photo of me, taken in 1959 in Nice, France, that Hendrik must have used as a bookmark. I was 23 years old. In the photo I'm leaning against a low wall looking down at the pavement; behind me the Mediterranean, vaguely visible in the distance. I'm wearing a wide skirted floral dress, more appropriate for an evening event than travelling, and black high heel sandals. My dark brown curled hair is shoulder length and I'm holding his jacket.

That photo opened a cache of memories, long forgotten, that took me back to how Hendrik and I, newly married, went on a journey that would take us in a direction we never expected.

We were married in February 1959. Before that, Hendrik had tried unsuccessfully to get his PhD in New Testament at the University of Pretoria. His dissertation proposal was summarily rejected by the faculty—all members of the ultra-conservative Dutch Reformed Church—as "too radical!"

He was not deterred by this setback. Instead he applied for a grant to the Alexander von Humboldt Foundation, or AvH, sponsored by the German Government and was accepted. The stipend would cover his studies at the University of Bonn, and living expenses.

The stipend, however, did not cover the costs of airplane tickets for our travel to Germany. We had nothing. Hendrik's parents, who were farmers, had given us two young heifers as a wedding gift and offered to sell them to pay for Hendrik's airplane ticket. My father paid for mine.

We booked our flight on a new South African airline company called Trek Airways. The price of the tickets allowed the company to use small propeller airplanes to transport about fifty passengers, fly only during the day, land in the afternoon to allow for some sightseeing, spend the night in a luxury hotel, then travel on to the next city the following day. It would take four days to get to Germany, but we were very happy with this plan.

We boarded the plane in late summer 1959. It turned out to be a journey of "firsts" for us. We flew from Johannesburg to Uganda. A bus took us from Entebbe Airport to the outskirts of Kampala, where we spent the night in a luxury one story hotel with cool porches, and nestled in a lush tropical garden. The peaceful quiet garden was a relief from the hours of constant engine drone of the airplane. That evening in the dining room I experienced my first culture shock. About a quarter of the guests were black. At the table next to us sat five black men, nattily dressed in business suits, talking in a strange language I didn't recognize. To the waiter, however, they spoke in perfect English.

"Did you see how many blacks there are here?" I whispered to Hendrik.

"Yes," he replied calmly, "It means you are no longer in South Africa."

Of course, I thought. In Uganda the social mix of black and white was an acceptable way of life.

Our next stop was Cairo, Egypt. The bus trip of several miles from the airport to the inner city was a nerve racking experience. Everyone drove at breakneck speed. Everyone sounded their horns for the other driver to get out of the way! It was a cacophony of sound that followed us right up to the entrance of the Nile Hilton on the banks of the Nile River.

Our suite of bedroom, sitting area, bathroom and balcony was on the sixth floor, away from the noisy city streets below. From our balcony we had a breathtaking view of the wide Nile River and the pyramids in the distance.

I was surrounded by sumptuous luxury. The sparkling white bathroom had all the amenities one could wish for: from bidet to blue fluffy towels and blue soap. The heady perfume of the soap whispered orient, mystery, romance. No French perfume came close to it. I was hooked.

The dining room was opulent, the food exquisite. And there I had my first taste of mango ice cream. I wallowed in all this luxury till Hendrik, ever the pragmatist, put a damper on my euphoria by commenting, "All this opulence borders on decadence. Think of all the people in the streets not far away from here who live in shacks and have hardly anything to eat." I felt guilty. This did not prevent him, I noticed, of relishing every morsel of his dinner and even ordering an extra dish of mango ice cream.

We had a chance during the afternoon to go on a tour to see the pyramids. Before we got off the bus the tour guide warned us against a horde of pickpockets and panhandlers. We saw them there, sitting on the desert sand like a pride of lions waiting for their prey. Luckily a few policemen were there to protect us.

Two men did manage to lure some money out of our pockets. For a few coins, they said, they would demonstrate how one could run up to the top of the pyramid and down again in five minutes! It was quite remarkable to watch them scale the man-high blocks of stone and down again.

When we left Cairo the next morning I didn't bother to tell Hendrik that I had sneaked all the bars of blue soap from the bathroom without feeling the least bit guilty.

Our next stop was Nice, France—where Hendrik took the photo of me. Except for one embarrassing incident and my first view of the Mediterranean, I don't remember anything about the city, where the hotel was or what food we ate.

We were on the bus the next day ready to leave for the airport, when a staff member of the hotel got on the bus.

She held up a sheer sky blue night gown and asked, "Does this belong to someone?"

I felt myself get red in the face as I raised my hand and said, "It's mine."

Loud laughter filled the bus. Hendrik laughed the loudest. From the back of the bus a man's voice shouted "Woo-Hoo." Thoroughly embarrassed I kept my head down till we reached the airport.

Our last stop was Paris where we managed to see most of the usual tourist attractions: The Eiffel Tower, Napoleon's tomb, Notre Dame, ending with a walk around the Place de Concorde munching on dry baguette, a discovery that spelled France to us.

From Paris we took a train to Munich where we attended the Goethe Institute near the rural village of Ebersberg, to learn German. Students came from a variety of countries like India, Jordan, Thailand, Turkey, Syria, Morocco, Sudan, Finland, USA, Greece and South Africa. We both passed the final exams. Hendrik was more proficient in grammar but hardly fluent. I, frustrated by the complicated grammar, became more familiar with the vernacular and fluent by reading every magazine and newspaper I could lay my hands on.

Our final destination was Bonn, the capital of Germany at that time, where we would stay for the next three and a half years.

A new phase in our life had begun. Little did we know when we began our journey that we would never return to South Africa, except to visit. And in another unanticipated way, a new life was developing and changed ours forever. I was pregnant.

Our daughter Greta was born August 15, 1960. The doctors' fee and hospital expenses were generously paid for by the German Government and, to our surprise, Greta was entitled to citizenship and a passport.

She was a year old when Hendrik and I met a charming elderly couple, Will and Kit Beardslee, at a reception for new stipendium candidates of the AvH. Foundation. Will was a professor of New Testament on sabbatical leave from Emory University, and he and Hendrik took to each other immediately: Will as mentor, Hendrik as eager student.

The following year Hendrik had completed his dissertation and passed his doctoral exams *summa cum laude*. We went back to South Africa with no job prospects and no money to live on. My parents took us in till Hendrik found a job a month later as roving reporter at the Department of Agriculture in Pretoria. Within a week we found and signed a lease for a small apartment. When we got back home my mother told us that a telegram from the USA had arrived at his parents' house and he should call them immediately. It was from the Dean at the School of Theology at Emory offering him a job as assistant professor of New Testament and a salary of $6,500.00 per year. Will Beardslee had done his job as mentor. Four months later, on August 25, 1962 we arrived in Atlanta with our future secured for good.

NOTE:

After I finished writing this story I reflected on how Providence sometimes steers our lives in a way we never envisioned. I find myself forever grateful to that ultra conservative faculty at the University of Pretoria for rejecting Hendrik's "too radical" dissertation proposal.

Remembering a Husband

Robert Browning wrote: "Grow old along with me! The best is yet to be." Idyllic words that conjure up an image of two old people sitting on rocking chairs on a porch, holding hands, watching the sun set.

We started out that way my husband Hendrik and I, secure in the thought that someday in the distant future we would deal with inevitable death, just not now. But life doesn't always play it that way. Suddenly he is diagnosed with a debilitating disease, Parkinson's, that will slowly turn his healthy body into a helpless wreck.

"Grow old along with me," becomes "I will grow old alone," and "the best is yet to be," becomes, "the best is now!"

We talked about the immediate future and how to keep him independent as long as possible. Then he began to struggle with washing himself, tying his shoes, getting out of a chair. I hovered anxiously, offering to help. It irritated him.

"I can do this, just give me time."

I tried another tactic, reminding him that I have a degree in nursing and he is the worst damn patient I've ever come across. I started to boss him around, it made him laugh. I joked while I dressed him, and so we went on, laughing through the pain.

But I also had to ask the painful questions. What do we do with his books? He told me who of his former students to give first choice to, the rest is up to me. The valuable carpenter tools in his workshop? His daughters have first claim there. And the most painful question: What to do with his ashes. He was adamant; no funeral, no memorial service.

His answer: "Do what you want, throw them in the creek, I don't care."

It hurt me that he reacted this way but I understood that another answer would bring the reality of inevitable death too close.

Then fate struck another blow. It was January 6th, the day of Epiphany, when I heard him call my name, and watched in horror as he tumbled down the stairs in our house. He was unconscious and blood seeped from his skull into the carpet. I called 911 and an ambulance rushed him to the trauma center in mid-town where six long hours later the neurosurgeon told me that brain surgery was not successful, that he was dying and on a respirator. I had to give permission to stop the machine. I consulted with my daughters and we tearfully agreed that he would want it so. Our only consolation: Providence gave him a quick way out of what would otherwise have been an agonizingly slow death.

But worse was yet to come. One day, long before illness took hold, he said, "Ida my love, I am going out on the cheap." He had arranged it all. Did he ever think through how that would be? They put his mangled body in a cardboard box for cremation. It was a severe shock for us, his family and close friends.

We were a small group of six who followed the hearse to the crematorium. There we walked into hell. It reminded me of Holocaust photos: stark brick walls, buckets on the floor, jugs on a dirty sink and the oven with its gaping door. The official apologized sheepishly for how it looked; nobody, it seemed, came to the crematorium.

Hendrik's best friend said a prayer of farewell when they pushed the box into the oven. The official told us, "It will take three hours; you can pick up the ashes in a few days." Our little group of mourners sought solace in the warm sun outside.

There was a memorial service after all. "He's not here to stop it," said a friend.

Colleagues, former students, friends, family all gathered in the university chapel to pay tribute to man of integrity and humility, always in fierce pursuit of the truth and academic excellence. Hendrik was born on February 3rd 1928 and 79 years old when he died in 2007.

Travelling Beyond Borders

Former students, most of them professors then, told of the impact he had on them and amusing stories, his malapropisms in class, "You can lead a horse to water, but you can't drink it for him." (What people probably did not understand is that a teacher can teach only so much; it is up to the student to make it work.) A daughter read a poem dedicated to her father: "A Birthday Poem for a Semiotician." It was the only time I wept in public. For almost three hours there was a spontaneous joyous celebration of a life well lived. Afterwards, almost a hundred people gathered at our house to eat and drink some of his favorite food and wine.

That was his only request: "Have a party!"

There was an avalanche of cards, telephone calls and visitors bringing food, flowers and their own stories of him. I was overwhelmed, my daughters too.

Archbishop Desmond Tutu sent flowers, "*Met baie liefde*," (with much love) all the way from South Africa. They reminded me of a time not so long ago when he sat in our kitchen eating corn meal porridge that my husband cooked, just like the porridge they ate as children. Fried sausages and South African wine completed their meal.

They shared boyhood stories: Tutu, the son of a black schoolteacher, taunted by whites as a child when he went to buy the "white man's newspaper" for his father. Growing up in a family where they learned tolerance for their white oppressors. My husband, the son of a poor white farmer, who in early childhood had no shoes in winter and only porridge three times a day, was taunted by whites because his playmates were black and his best friend Jewish. His parents set an example of treating people of all colors with respect and care and to communicate in Zulu with the black people who lived on their farm.

They talked about how they came to study Theology: Tutu who would later become Archbishop of the Anglican Church in South Africa, and by promoting peaceful reconciliation when Apartheid ended, recipient of the Nobel Peace prize; my husband, breaking his ties with the ultra-conservative Dutch Reformed Church in South Africa to end up as a professor at Emory in the USA.

There was one more thing to do: planning the "last rites" as I called them, with my three daughters. We took the ashes of a beloved husband and father to the Smokey Mountains, a place he loved to visit; choosing the more remote areas where few tourists came, where we walked in the woods that gave shelter to flowering Rhododendron or enjoyed the view of a wide grassy space, a log cabin in the distance a reminder that this was once a farm, and in the early morning quiet breathed in the fresh clean air after a rain storm. A river, flowing wide and strong through the forest is where we wanted to scatter his ashes.

It was a balmy, sunny day in early May; the trees were covered in soft spring green. Early wildflowers grew along the path that took us to the peaceful spot close to the river bank that we chose for our ritual. We stood in a circle, holding hands, the container with his ashes at our feet and silently said our goodbye. Two Canada geese sat on a rock almost in the middle of the river watching what we did.

Earlier in the day we decided that we each wanted to keep a few ounces of his ashes. On the river bank we scooped some in small paper cups. One daughter worried about her father's ashes in a paper cup. I reassured her; with his ironic sense of humor, he would have loved it. Then we threw a hundred shrub roses in shades of red, purple and yellow, sent by a loving son-in-law, in the water. "To pave the way," one daughter said.

We took turns scattering the ashes, throwing small bundles of long stemmed yellow roses after. Some of the ashes sank to the bottom, but it didn't matter. Nature would take care of it with time.

When we were done we saw that all the roses were gone except three yellow ones that were stuck in a branch of a dead tree lying in the water. Suddenly one of the geese on the rock got in the water and paddled over to the branch, pecked and pulled at one of the roses until it floated free. Then it paddled back to the rock. I knew, the goose was just curious but for me it was a symbolic act, as if the rose was my husband's spirit, set free, and sent home.

Afterwards, we sat on the balcony of the hotel that overlooked the same river further down. We sipped champagne and ate strawberries in celebration of our life with a loving husband and father. We talked about the good times and, yes, about the not so good times, but of those there were not too many. It was all part of the grieving process. I was moved by how attuned the four of us were, and I knew he would have been quietly happy of all we did on that day.

A few days after we returned form the Smokey Mountains I went to Hendrik's workshop to find something.

No other room in this house evokes so many memories of Hendrik than his workshop. He was a successful scholar in his field of Theology, but it's in the workshop that his many talents: carpenter, electrician, plumber and all round fixer of broken things came to light. Anything from leaking faucets, to obnoxious computers was restored under his capable hands.

Since his untimely death, the workshop was rarely used. It had become a room to dump empty boxes, broken lamps and other, I don't know-what-to-do-with-this, stuff.

One day in the early summer, I went there to find a tool and suddenly realized how unhappy Hendrik would be to see the state of his workshop. I felt ashamed and guilty and decided then and there to begin a major cleanup.

Hendrik was a "saver"—"hoarder" conjures up someone living in an accumulation of trash. His workshop, however, was a well-organized workplace. Old doors—to convert into tables—were stacked in a corner. Shelves, reaching from ceiling to basement floor, held rows of cleaned marmalade jars, filled with nails, screws and other small items saved up through the years. On the wall above a ten foot workbench hung a collection of hammers, screwdrivers of all sizes and other tools that any professional carpenter, electrician or plumber would envy.

Next to the workbench a radial arm saw rested on a specially built table. With it he made bookcases, desks for his three daughters, loudspeaker boxes for his HiFi system and expanded our living space in the basement—which has windows on three sides—with two bedrooms, a bathroom (which included a septic tank) and large laundry room where I could also do my sewing. All the leftover wood was stored under the workbench counter; smaller pieces, anything from twelve to two inches were neatly stacked on a shelf to be used another time.

This habit of saving began in early childhood. His father, a farmer in South Africa, went into severe debt during the depression, and the family was reduced to abject poverty. For some years Hendrik and his two siblings had no shoes, even in winter, when they trudged barefoot across frost covered fields to go to school in the small town three miles away. Their meals consisted of porridge and a little milk three times a day. Only on Sundays were they treated to a teaspoon of sugar, carefully measured, on their morning porridge. In their orchard they could only pick up fruit that had fallen to the ground. "Cut out the rotten part and eat the good part." The good fruit picked from the trees was sold on the market in town to add to their meager income.

It was then that "Save everything; you never know when you will need it," became a rule in their house and stayed with him for the rest of his life.

One near disastrous incident that happened some years ago proved how "save everything" was ingrained in Hendrik's brain. I was at work at Emory one morning when the phone rang. It was Hendrik, "You need to come home right now and take me to emergency at Dekalb General Hospital. I accidentally cut off the tip of my finger with the radial arm saw." I rushed home and found him waiting in the driveway, his right hand covered in a blood-soaked handkerchief. When we got to the hospital he said, "Drop me off at the door, go back home and bring the tip of my finger so the doctor can sew it back on."

I didn't have the courage to argue with him about the futility of such an errand, so I dutifully drove home to search for whatever was left of his finger.

I found a mess of useless bloody strips of skin and bone splinters mixed with sawdust which I carefully spooned into a small container—I knew better: to arrive at the hospital empty handed would cause me no end of trouble. I also sneaked in a mini bottle of his favorite Johnny Walker Scotch.

The hand-surgeon—who laughed and heartily approved my "medicinal" cure for shock—did a marvelous job of mending the shortened finger.

Hendrik took the loss of part of his finger stoically. "No need to cut a nail on this finger anymore."

He smiled a little sheepishly when I sometimes found him working with the radial saw and gently teased him to keep his fingers out of the way.

It took me over a week to clean more than five years of accumulated dust from the shelves. The marmalade jars standing three deep on several shelves were a testimony of all the years during our marriage when his never varied breakfast consisted of two slices of toast with marmalade, a glass of orange juice, and a cup of coffee.

In the back of one of the shelves I found a jar filled with rusted bent nails. "What did he save these for?" I wondered. But it took me back to the time when we first met.

I was an eighteen-year-old first year student at the University of Pretoria; he was 27 and working on his third degree, a Master's in philosophy. We often went for long walks around the neighborhood of the boarding house where we rented rooms. We talked about everything under the sun: our hopes and dreams, especially his of becoming a pastor one day, and the state of the world in general.

On one of these walks, he suddenly stopped in mid-sentence, picked up two rusty nails and threw them under the bushes along the sidewalk.

"Why did you do that?" I asked.

"Many blacks walk barefoot and might step on a nail and get hurt," he explained. That little act revealed to me the person he was and the pastor he would be; kind and caring.

Hendrik had a remarkable ability to concentrate on the job at hand: keeping track of hundreds of colored wires which he soldered together when he built his

Hi-Fi radio, and connecting it to a record player. One afternoon, soon after he got his first computer, I found him in his study—which was next to the workshop in the basement—with the innards of the new computer spread out on his desk.

"WHAT are you doing?" I asked.

"I just wanted to see what it looks like inside and how it works," he calmly replied. A few hours later the computer was restored and functioning beautifully. His in-depth knowledge of how computers worked became useful for the School of Theology. He guided all the secretaries through the process of switching from typewriter to using the computer, and showed many of his colleagues the benefit of using e-mail instead of handwritten notes.

His ability to focus intently on any job he had in mind also had a downside. Once he had figured out how to do something it was difficult to persuade him that his plan might not work and to do it differently. Like the tree he once wanted to cut down.

In his workshop he had all the paraphernalia for cutting down trees: a chainsaw—which I called "the monster," because it tempted Hendrik to tackle something much bigger than him—to weighted ropes for stabilizing a falling tree.

One day he called me to the backyard. "I want to cut down that tree," he said, pointing to a tree that leaned precariously over our neighbor's fence.

There stood Hendrik, a not very muscular 5 feet 7 inches and the Goliath tree almost thirty feet high.

"You're going to cut it down by yourself?" I asked, seeing nothing but disaster looming ahead.

"No, you have to help me," pointing to the weighted rope that he had fastened to a thick upper branch. "Hold on to the end. When the tree starts to come down, pull it towards you so it doesn't topple into the neighbor's yard."

"What if it falls on top of me?" I asked.

"Just jump out of the way when it starts to fall."

"You can't be serious," I said. "I don't have the strength to hold on to such a heavy weight."

"Go get the kids to help you." He meant our ten-year-old twin daughters.

That made me angry. "Are you crazy?" I yelled, "Forget it, I'm not going to put MY children into any danger." I walked away.

He called me back. "Okay, okay, I'll do it another way." He picked up the rope and fastened it to a sturdy pine tree nearby.

I stood watching at a safe distance while he sawed the tree. It came down with a crash hitting the pine tree in the process. I let out a cheer which made him smile. But I couldn't help pointing out too that the tree fell exactly where he had wanted me to stand with the rope. and that some of the heavy branches landed on top of my recently planted azalea bushes, destroying half of them.

"Oh, they'll grow back again," was all he said. (They did.)

The most vivid memory I have of Hendrik is the day I heard his calls for help from his workshop. By then he had been diagnosed with an unusual form of Parkinson's: losing his balance and falling without warning, and slowly losing the use of his left arm. I found him in his workshop wedged between the shelves and a small iron worktable in front. As always, when he fell, he needed help to get up.

"Were you trying to do something here?" I asked.

"No," he replied with a sigh, "Just looking at my tools."

A few days later, he fell again, this time down the stairs of our house. Six hours later he died in the hospital operating room of severe inoperable head injuries.

As I look back on the last year of his life that sad sentence, "Just looking at my tools," haunts me to this day.

He never complained. In my concern for his physical safety I sometimes failed to recognize the emotional battle he must have gone through while illness slowly, relentlessly, took away more and more of his faculties to create and fix things in his workshop, and from which his family and many friends so often benefited.

Endnotes

References:

Lost Trails of the Transvaal, T.V. Bulpin. Johannesburg, South Africa. Thomas Nelson and Sons, LTD, 1965, p. 1–2.

The Bantu-speaking Tribes of South Africa. Edited by I. Schapera. Cape Town, South Africa: Maskew Miller Limited, 1953. Photos from face p. 96, and face p. 120 Lobola reference p. 113.

Acknowledgements

I would like to thank my three daughters, Greta Gezina Boers, Johanna Hommes Boers, and Maria Boers Morris for preparing the manuscript and images.

My daughters and I are grateful to Lee Sorensen for his sensitive editing of several of the photographs, and to Svea Elisha for her elegant cover design.

Most importantly, I would like to thank all the members of my writers' group, *The Writers' Bloc*, who have encouraged my writing, and supported me over the years: Joseph Baird, Milt Crane, Jo Brachman, Sandy Gillespie, Jeffrey Holmes, Rife Hughey, Tom Painting, Lois Pippin, Judy Rogers, Sandra Rouse, and Richard Low. Special remembrance to Bard Lindeman, Charles Napravnik, and Trudy Kretchman, of blessed memory.

Made in the USA
Columbia, SC
10 November 2023